GIANT PANDAS

大
熊
猫

GIANT PANDAS

JOHN SEIDENSTICKER

SUSAN LUMPKIN

Collins

An Imprint of HarperCollinsPublishers

HarperCollins books may be purchased for
educational, business or sales promotional use.
For information, please write:
Special Markets Department
HarperCollins Publishers
10 East 53rd Street
New York, NY 10022.

FIRST EDITION

The name of the "Smithsonian," "Smithsonian Institution" and
the sunburst logo are registered trademarks of the Smithsonian
Institution.

Designed by Linda McKnight of McKnight Design, LLC
Edited by Suzanne Fox of Red Bird Publishing, Inc.

Printed on acid-free paper.

Library of Congress Cataloging-in-Publication Data

Lumpkin, Susan.
    Giant pandas / Susan Lumpkin, John Seidensticker.—1st ed.
        p. cm.
    Da xiong mao Cover title also in Chinese:
    ISBN: 978-0-06-120578-1
    ISBN-10: 0-06-120578-8
1. Giant panda. I. Seidensticker, John. II. Title. III. Title: Cover
title also in Chinese.

QL737.C214L85 2007
599.789—dc22   2006051866

07   08   09   10   11   TP   10   9   8   7   6   5   4   3   2   1

CONTENTS

4 RAISING
BABIES
98

5 SAVING THE
GIANT PANDA
132

The Incomparable Tai Shan

Googling Tai Shan, the giant panda born at the Smithsonian's National Zoo, on his first birthday on July 9, 2006, resulted in more than 72,000 hits. Twenty-seven thousand people, including media from around the world, turned out for his birthday party at the zoo. The birthday cake was delivered by FedEx. The cake was for human consumption, so Tai Shan celebrated with a giant frozen ice treat topped with a huge number "1." When Tai Shan first appeared before his adoring public that morning, the crowd spontaneously sang "Happy Birthday."

Since his birth, Tai Shan had been an international superstar, a royal animal that his keepers called "His Highness" and "Wild Child." More than 200,000 people voted for the zoo's selection of Chinese names, and Tai Shan, or "Peaceful Mountain," won, though many bloggers campaigned vigorously for "Butterstick," because a newborn panda is about the size of a stick of butter. Via television, radio and the zoo's website, countless millions heard his name announced on his 100th day, following a Chinese tradition of naming human babies on that day. Tai Shan's birth, naming, his first steps, public debut, first venture outside, birthday and his every veterinary exam were reported as breaking news across the country, if not around the world.

Tai Shan, the National Zoo's first surviving giant panda cub, stole the hearts of people across the country and around the world. Millions of fans who couldn't visit him in person watched his every move via webcams.

Many human mothers marveled at and sympathized with giant panda mother Mei Xiang, who offered Tai Shan such devoted care, and delighted in tracking Tai Shan's development from helpless newborn to robust cub.

The zoo's panda webcam, which offered views of Tai Shan and his mother Mei Xiang around the clock starting the day after he was born, attracted some 21 million visits in his first year. On at least two occasions, the sheer number of people trying to log onto the website overwhelmed the servers for the entire Smithsonian Institution. People sent thousands of emails, expressing admiration and thanks, and instantly alerting zoo staff when they thought something was amiss. In the days after Tai Shan was born, some people tracked the cams so persistently that they noticed Mei Xiang hadn't eliminated for several days after giving birth, which is perfectly normal panda behavior.

Visitors also flocked to the Fujifilm Giant Panda Habitat

at the zoo to see "the cutest cub in the world." Among these were First Lady Laura Bush and a host of politicians, celebrities including Nicole Kidman, and even the Queen of Bhutan.

Tai Shan was not the first giant panda born in the United States. That distinction belongs to Hua Mei ("China/USA"), born in the summer of 1999 at the San Diego Zoo, followed by Mei Sheng ("Born in the USA" or "Beautiful Life") in 2003 and Su Lin ("A little bit of something very cute") in 2005, about a month after Tai Shan. A friendly bi-coastal rivalry emerged over

Everything that makes an adult giant panda so appealing—a round, large head, clumsy appearance, eyes that look very large—is exaggerated in a cub, making even the most reserved person exclaim, "He's soooo cute!"

which was the cuter and smarter panda cub, although most agreed it was probably a draw—a baby panda is just plain cute. Still, Tai Shan seems to attract the lion's share of national and international attention. He and his mother graced the cover of the July 2006 *National Geographic* and Tai Shan was regularly on the front page of *The Washington Post*. The Washington Mystics, the local women's basketball team, made a giant panda the team's mascot, and many Washingtonians want the District of Columbia's official animal to be a giant panda rather than a native species such as the bald eagle.

The zoo's pandas have also attracted significant donations. Fujifilm committed $7.8 million to the zoo's Giant Panda Conservation Program, which funded an expanded new home for the trio that opened in the fall of 2006, education and science programs built around giant pandas, and helped defray the zoo's annual $1 million contribution to China's giant panda program, an amount that increased by $600,000 per year since Tai Shan's birth. Animal Planet made a large contribution as well, as did FedEx, and several individual donors. In addition, many other businesses both national and local offered support.

All of these, plus significant federal dollars, enable the zoo's panda family to live a life of luxury, with plenty of bamboo delivered fresh daily, air-conditioned digs, unrivalled veterinary care, and, of course, pampering keepers. Scientists study their behavior, monitor their diet and their stress levels and artificially inseminated Mei Xiang when she and Tian Tian failed to mate in early 2005.

How did an animal with no particular historical significance in China, that no westerner had ever heard of before 1869 or seen

Once Tai Shan ventured outdoors, he spent much of his time up in a tree. This behavior helps protect cubs in the wild from predators. There is no such risk in a zoo, where keepers carefully protect their charges.

Surprisingly, giant pandas did not acquire cult-figure status in China and weren't even very well known there until they became valuable to westerners. Now, however, giant pandas have come to symbolize China in western eyes.

"Pandarazzi" follow pandas like paparazzi follow human celebrities.

alive until 1916, become a cultural demi-god? Giant pandas have become the world's most esteemed animals, achieving a status that may be comparable to the cat in cults of ancient Egypt.

The question is, why? Every zoo outside of China that has ever exhibited giant pandas has been overwhelmed by people clamoring to see them. The animals are treated like royalty—no other zoo animals have such lavish habitats or so much attention devoted to satisfying their every need. Airplanes materialize when one must be moved. The media cover their actions like paparazzi stalk Angelina Jolie and Brad Pitt.

People mourn when a giant panda they know dies, feeling the loss deeply. When Ling-Ling and then Hsing-Hsing died at the National Zoo, the media recounted their lives, the details of their deaths and the effects of their absence on the human community, treatment accorded only a handful of people. Ling-Ling died in the same week as ballet legend Rudolf Nureyev, and both were eulogized in print and on the air in roughly equal measure. It's as if giant pandas are people too, but more so. Cynically, the four-star hotels and other deluxe enclaves frequented by westerners in China are called "panda houses"; some Chinese resent the fact that zoo giant pandas may have it better than they do.

What makes giant pandas the most charismatic of the mega-vertebrates? Scholars have combed the arts and literature of China for evidence of an ancient affinity between people and giant pandas. This search has yielded just a few dozen written references, and the record in the arts is sparser still. While Chinese art is replete with bears, bamboo and the misty mountain landscapes giant

Whether he is playing limbo under a tree limb or sleeping, few moments of Tai Shan's life have not been documented in photographs or on video. Many fans have created web pages to display their images.

(Bottom) Apart from its intrinsic value, a baby panda born in a U.S. zoo increases the contribution the zoo must make to China to support giant panda conservation there. But each baby is priceless in terms of building the size of the zoo panda population.

(Opposite) Seemingly tender moments between giant pandas make it easy to succumb to the animals' charm. Although adult giant pandas appear as helpless as young ones, they are capable of hurting and even killing a human adult.

pandas inhabit, no pandas are depicted until the 20th century. One of China's earliest art critics (ca. 847) wrote, "Pictures contain the greatest treasures of the empire." This suggests that giant pandas were not considered "rare and precious animals" and "national treasures," as they are officially designated today.

In their book *The Giant Panda*, Ramona and Desmond Morris cite several reasons for the giant panda's cult status. First, pandas have features that resemble those of humans: flat faces, short tails, sitting upright, "thumbs" and sex organs hidden from view. Furthermore, most of us gush and coo over babies, and a giant panda looks like an infant—the flat face, disproportionately large eyes in a disproportionately large head, playfulness, apparent clumsiness, the appearance of softness, a round outline, a short cute name, a need for protection. Next, giant pandas are big but seemingly harmless to people and, with their bamboo diet, to other animals as well. In a category by itself are the giant panda's striking markings. Then there is the overall panda mystique: It is rare, it lives like a hermit in misty mountains and the history of its discovery is romantic, full of drama and danger. And giant pandas are valuable in terms of dollars and cents. People like that.

Finally, the Morrises suggest that the popularity of teddy bears prepared people to love a "super teddy bear." The teddy bear first appeared in the United States in 1904, named after President Theodore Roosevelt. The toy bears were first sold in a New York novelty store,

but soon retail giant Sears Roebuck was also selling them.

Lots of people and things—from Bob Jones to Beanie Babies—suddenly attract a large and devoted, sometimes fanatical following, for reasons that leave many of us scratching our heads. A young giant panda named Ming arrived at the London Zoo at the end of 1938, just as war was breaking out in Europe, and died there at the end of 1944. During this terrible time, "she became something of a symbol—a bit of fun in a funless, burning city." A few years earlier, the baby panda Su Lin arrived in the U.S. in the dark days of the Depression and had the entire country at his feet. Hsing-Hsing and Ling-Ling captured rapt attention in 1972 in a nation suffering disunity and trauma because of the Vietnam War. Most recently, the giant pandas brought to the United States may be welcome distractions from our increasingly fractious politics and sometimes dangerous society.

A Priest and His Black-and-White Bear

Giant pandas did not begin their meteoric rise to superstardom until about 130 years ago, when the French missionary Père Armand David sent the first specimen from Muping in western Sichuan to the Paris Natural History Museum. In a description sent to the museum's director, the intrepid naturalist-priest called the black-and-white bear "easily the prettiest kind of animal I know." Père David's instant admiration presaged the widespread adulation to come.

Père David was among the first westerners to penetrate the closed Middle Kingdom, which had long been hostile to foreigners. At the time, the western public closely tracked the exploits of their explorers, and any new find attracted attention.

A bouquet of flowers and a child's touch create the illusion that pandas are like kindly uncles. Standing upright, this costumed-character panda enhances the sense that "pandas are people too."

Père David's deer, *Elaphurus davidianus,* was named for the intrepid French priest-naturalist who spirited the western world's first specimens of this species out of the Imperial Palace in Beijing.

Père David

Père Armand David (1826-1900), a French Basque by birth and a Lazarist missionary priest by vocation, was sent to China to save souls in 1862, where he lived and traveled for the next decade. With his passion and talent for natural history, he also undertook to save specimens of China's wildlife. He was lucky to have arrived in China just after western gunboats compelled the isolationist Chinese rulers to open the interior to foreigners in 1860. Brave, perhaps foolhardy, and certainly arrogantly western, he faced down bandits, illnesses and other hardships to carry out his mission of collecting and naming animals. He was warned, for instance, against traveling to Muping, where he was to find the west's first giant panda. He wrote in his diary, "I am told of thefts and murders committed by bands of brigands. But if I am to be held back by fears of this kind I can do no exploring, since the wild places, reputed to be the haunts of thieves and malefactors, are precisely the ones that offer the most in the way of natural history in China. . . . I shall be careful to keep my gun much in evidence."

While this remarkable man will forever be linked in the public's mind with giant pandas, biologists recognize him for the countless other species he brought to scientific attention during his explorations of the edges of the Celestial Empire. These include golden monkeys, serow and other mammals, 58 birds, about 100 insects, many snails and fish and the Chinese giant salamander, one of many species named for him. David was also a prodigious plant collector, and many plants were named in his honor: dove tree, *Davidia involucrata*; butterfly bush, *Buddleia davidii*; a clematis *Clematis heracleifolia var. davidiana*; a lily, *Lilium davidi*; a peach, *Prunus davidiana*; and a photinia, *Photinia davidiana*, to name a few.

But many years passed before pandamania truly caught fire. With only a handful of specimens in western museums, mostly in Paris, and no new information coming out of China, the black-and-white animal known in England as the parti-colored bear was virtually unknown.

All this changed about 1900, when a scientist at the British

The red panda was known in the west long before the giant panda was. After the giant panda was discovered, this species was often called the lesser panda. We now know that the two are not closely related.

The ancestors of these modern Yi people, one of several Tibetan minority groups living in the mountains of Sichuan and nearby provinces, likely ran into western explorers looking for giant pandas there.

Museum examined a skull and assorted limb bones and concluded that they belonged not to a bear at all, but to a relative of the red panda. He renamed the parti-colored bear the "great panda," and moved the museum's specimens out of the bear gallery. Other naturalists had earlier come to this erroneous conclusion, but for some reason giving the rare and unusual animal a catchy new name created a buzz. Adventurers soon determined to secure more specimens.

Despite numerous western scientific expeditions into giant panda country, it wasn't until 1916 that the first westerner saw one alive, and another 14 years passed before the next sighting. In an era when big-game hunters were celebrities, giant pandas became the ultimate trophy. First to take up the quest were Kermit and Theodore Roosevelt, Jr., the sons of the 26th President of the United States. Their China expedition was supported by the Field Museum in Chicago, which stood to be the first in the U.S. to possess a giant panda. After months of arduous travel through mountains rife with bandits, the brothers earned—with the invaluable help of the Yi, a Tibetan people—the dubious distinction of being the first westerners to shoot a giant panda. The press glorified their exploits and the American public was thrilled. Other museums sent expeditions, all wanting to display a stuffed giant panda. Still, by 1935, six westerners had shot only four pandas between them (the Roosevelt brothers took credit for a single giant panda, as did two other hunters). The toll on giant pandas was far greater, however, as local hunters killed many more to satisfy western demand. The Smithsonian's Museum of Natural History, for instance, obtained 15 skins and skeletons from an American missionary in Sichuan, who bought them from local hunters. Counting four animals killed for Père David, at least 42 giant pandas left China as piles of skin and bones.

Bring 'em Back Alive

Then in the 1930s, a couple of Americans began vying to bring a giant panda back alive. One was a famed hunter named Tangier Smith. His competitor was a New York socialite named Ruth Harkness, who picked up the torch after her giant-panda-seeking husband died in Shanghai. The conflict and competition between the hunter and the socialite was long and convoluted, but finally in 1936 Harkness, by fair means or foul, captured the gold: She made it to San Francisco with a baby giant panda named Su Lin. In San Francisco, Chicago and New York, huge crowds greeted them, clamoring to see the little cub Harkness fed with a bottle and carried in her arms like a child. The press covered the story relentlessly.

Ruth Harkness with panda cub Su Lin.

Curiously, Harkness struggled to find a zoo willing to meet her price for the cub. The zoo in Chicago balked, as did New York's Bronx Zoo. When Su Lin was offered to the National Zoo, Lucille Mann, wife of zoo Director William M. Mann, said, "We would have loved keeping it in Washington, but the astronomical price was far beyond the National Zoo's modest budget." Ultimately, Su Lin did find a home back at

Along with countless renditions of plush pandas, designers have fashioned panda likenesses into nearly every product imaginable—purses, backpacks, jewelry, even toasters. Such items are as common in China as they are in U.S. zoos.

Chicago's Brookfield Zoo, which sponsored Harkness' further collecting trips to China.

Su Lin spawned an entire industry of giant panda memorabilia, from plush toys and jewelry to cartoons and books. Universal Studios launched the animated cartoon character Andy Panda in 1939, and he starred in many features until 1949; in comic books, Andy lived until 1962. Perhaps inspired by the popular appeal of Su Lin, the first Curious George story was published in 1941, about a mischievous African monkey taken to a New York zoo. The immensely popular and long-running Babar series debuted in 1931 featuring a young African elephant brought to Paris, which experience later qualifies him to become King of

the Elephants. Giant panda products continue to be a booming business. The National Zoo Stores carry hundreds of panda items, from 30-cent postcards to $200 plush toys. In between are panda T-shirts, mouse pads, purses, mugs, jewelry and books.

More important, Su Lin so enchanted Americans and Europeans that he is credited with ending the practice of killing giant pandas for science or sport. The four Americans who had shot giant pandas set the example and vowed never to shoot another. But ending the carnage had less to do with

Sitting upright, his back to his admirers, this panda is oblivious to the concern people have for the future of his species. For pandas, the good life mainly consists of plenty of bamboo.

conservation than with an emotional response to a charming individual. Indeed, Su Lin's wild popularity spurred zoos' efforts to obtain more giant pandas for their adoring public, though this was often as lethal to pandas as a shotgun. In 1939, Tangier Smith captured nine giant pandas, only five of which reached London alive, where yet another soon died. There was concern in some quarters that giant pandas were disappearing in the wild because local hunters continued to fill the markets of Chengdu with animals both dead and alive. One observer used this glutted market to claim that pandas were not rare all.

But zoo directors still wanted to hitch their star to this rising celebrity. Such was the western desire for pandas that even World War II only slowed, didn't stop, the panda exodus from China. Between 1937 and 1946, a total of 14 giant pandas arrived alive in Western zoos. No one knows how many died en route. And none lived very long by modern standards, or ever bred. Civil war in China, followed by the formation of the People's Republic in 1949, finally ended the drain. The last giant panda in the west, and the last in a zoo anywhere including China, died at the Brookfield Zoo in 1953. China allowed no exports again until a few animals went to Europe in 1957 and 1959, but quickly stopped them despite the continued pleas of European zoos. (With no diplomatic relations between the two nations, U.S. zoos could not even consider trading with China.) For the next 14 years, China held fast to the giant pandas, releasing a few animals only to North Korea, a secretive nation from which news rarely emerged.

Giant Panda Diplomacy

In a bold, unexpected move, U.S. President Richard M. Nixon

Modern zoo digs for giant pandas are more like palaces than the old-style cages once typical of zoos. Naturalistic outdoor habitats and spacious indoor enclosures are designed to meet all the giant pandas' needs.

(Bottom) Richard and Patricia Nixon, the President and First Lady of the Unites States, brought the first giant pandas to the National Zoo in 1972, following Nixon's historic diplomatic mission to reopen relations in China.

(Opposite) Giant pandas in zoos outside of China are ambassadors for their wild relatives, helping to create awareness about their struggle for survival in the face of ever-increasing human intrusion into their natural habitat.

met with People's Republic of China Chairman Mao Zedong in 1972 to mend the long rift between the two countries. This historic event was quickly overshadowed by some really big news: As a gesture of friendship, the P.R.C. would send a pair of giant pandas to the United States; the U.S. would reciprocate with a pair of Alaskan musk oxen named Milton and Matilda. Ling-Ling and Hsing-Hsing became the world's most famous diplomats. For months American zoos lobbied for ownership of the exotic immigrants. The President finally bestowed them on the National Zoo, as befitting a gift to the people of the United States. For the next 26 years, Ling-Ling and Hsing-Hsing reigned supreme as the only giant pandas in the United States. And behind the scenes, the giant pandas' gift inaugurated a scientific collaboration between National Zoo and Chinese biologists that remains strong.

China continued to send giant pandas as diplomats to Tokyo, Paris, London, Mexico City, Madrid and Berlin. With a growing awareness of the worldwide wildlife conservation crisis, giant pandas also came to symbolize endangered species. It is telling that when Ling-Ling and Hsing-Hsing came to the National Zoo in 1972, no news account mentioned that they were endangered, even through the World Wildlife Fund had adopted the giant panda as its logo in 1961. Today, no news account would omit that fact.

(Top) Giant pandas have come to symbolize the importance of wildlife conservation. Giant pandas grace the logos of conservation organizations, including Friends of the National Zoo and the World Wildlife Fund.

(Opposite) Giant pandas can only be imported into the United States for zoo exhibits under special conditions to ensure that the species is not exploited for commercial gain. One requirement is that zoos support panda conservation in the wild.

Of course, it is always possible to love something too much. In the 1980s, as zoos everywhere sought to display giant pandas, China stopped giving them. Instead, short-term exhibition loans were made for which zoos paid $100,000 a month, money easily recovered with admission fees. Soon the situation was getting out of hand. Zoos as well as Disney World and the Michigan State Fair were lining up to rent a panda. These traveling animals were precluded from breeding, so apart from some questionable educational value, the loans did nothing to contribute to giant panda conservation, and may have even been detrimental to efforts to increase zoo populations.

With giant pandas protected under the U.S. Endangered Species Act in 1984, and listed on the Convention on International Trade in Endangered Species (CITES), the U.S. Fish and Wildlife Service (FWS) banned imports of giant pandas in 1988. In 1990, the international conservation community also recommended a temporary ban on all giant panda loans. Under intense political pressure, and amid lawsuits and censure by the Zoo and Aquarium Association (AZA), an import permit allowed the Columbus Zoo to rent two male pandas in 1992, but only because the money for the loan created a new giant panda reserve in China. A lawsuit was brought by the World Wildlife Fund and the AZA against the U.S. Department of the Interior, pressing it to review giant panda loan policy and ensure that the loans complied with CITES and the Endangered Species Act. This meant the loans must not be detrimental to the pandas in

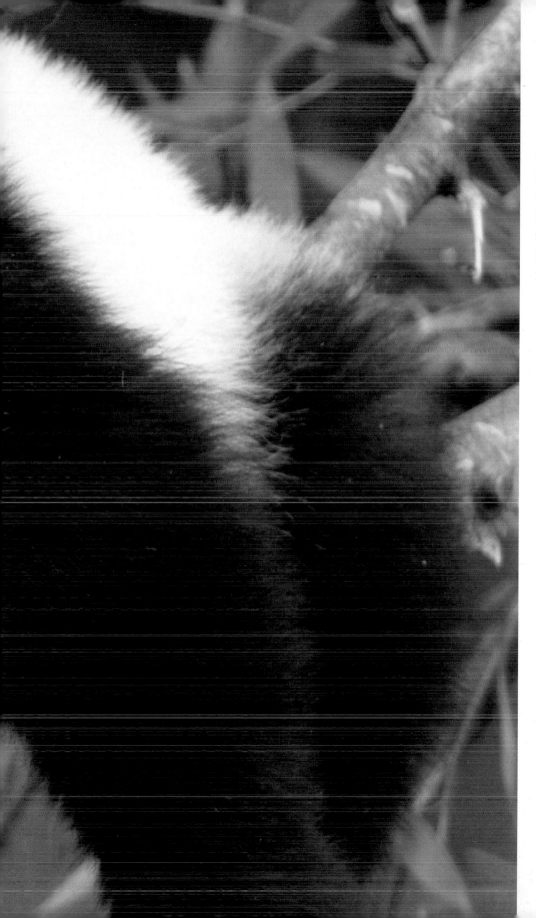

Giant pandas now live at four
zoos in the United States—the
National Zoo, the San Diego
Zoological Park, Zoo Atlanta, and
the Memphis Zoo. So far, pandas
have bred at all but the Memphis
Zoo.

The 2005 birth of the National Zoo's Tai Shan, a male, was closely followed by a birth of a female at the San Diego Zoo. A female was born at Zoo Atlanta about a year later.

the wild, must enhance the conservation of wild pandas, and must not be primarily for commercial purposes.

A moratorium on panda loans went into effect in 1993 to allow the FWS to review its policy. It was lifted only in 1998, when the San Diego Zoo was awarded a permit and welcomed Shi Shi and Bai Yun. This zoo had applied for its permit before the moratorium so their permit was "grandfathered" but it is complying with the new policy. A year later, Zoo Atlanta received a permit to import Lun Lun and Yang Yang. And in 2000, the National Zoo submitted its application. Ling-Ling had died in 1992, Hsing-Hsing in 1999. For the first time in 27 years, no giant panda lived in Washington, D.C. Though there were giant pandas in California and Georgia, people wanted them in the nation's capital. The FWS issued the permit in October 2000, and soon Mei Xiang and Tian Tian were FedExed to Dulles International Airport. In 2003, the Memphis Zoo became the fourth U.S. zoo to boast a pair of pandas; Ya Ya and Le Le arrived there by FedEx as well.

These panda loans were approved only because each zoo has committed to long-term research and conservation programs to enhance the survival of giant pandas in the wild. Moreover, China has agreed to use the loan funds to support giant panda conservation. The National Zoo's agreement includes a monetary contribution and research, conservation and educational initiatives for giant pandas in the wild and in zoos. A major portion of the research programs is devoted to increasing the number of giant pandas in zoos to create a self-sustaining population, a sort of insurance policy against the

species' extinction in the wild. But the overarching goal is to ensure that the policy never has to pay out.

Incentives for Conservation

When the giant panda first emerged on the world scene, its range in China had been shrinking for centuries. So while the western obsession with giant pandas enhanced their symbolic and monetary value to the Chinese, it also created an incentive for their conservation. The first evidence of this came in 1939, when the government of Sichuan briefly forbade the capture of giant pandas, perhaps the first wildlife conservation regulation in China. In 1946, a Chinese newspaper voiced fears that the market would drive giant pandas into extinction. The new People's Republic of China, established in 1949 when the Communist Party came to power, allowed no panda exports for nearly a decade, then explicitly addressed issues of giant panda conservation in 1962, when giant pandas were protected and hunting banned. In 1963, the first three giant panda reserves were established, growing to 13 by 1989 and to more than 60 today. Setting aside land for reserves came at great social and economic cost. In Tangjiahe Reserve, an entire logging operation was shut down and the farming commune that supported it resettled.

National Zoo scientists collaborate with their Chinese colleagues to improve the health and reproduction of giant pandas in Chinese breeding centers such as that at Wolong in Sichuan province.

In 1941, two giant pandas en route to the U.S. stayed briefly in Chongqing in eastern Sichuan. They were visited by thousands of local residents, only a few of whom had ever seen a panda before. It wasn't until the 1950s that giant pandas began to appear in Chinese zoos. And in 1963, a pair at the Beijing Zoo produced the first zoo-born giant panda; in 1978, a panda was

born by artificial insemination. Before American zoos were even thinking about conservation breeding programs, the Chinese were conducting one. The Chengdu Research Base of Giant Panda Breeding on the outskirts of Sichuan's largest city and the breeding facility at Wolong Giant Panda Reserve testify to their ongoing commitment, and their success is growing rapidly. National Zoo reproductive physiologists David Wildt, Jo Gayle Howard and others, including many Chinese colleagues, have been working to improve breeding performance in China's captive pandas by, among other things, improving procedures for preserving semen and artificial insemination.

John Seidensticker and two Smithsonian colleagues traveled to three giant panda reserves in 1981, among the first westerners to visit these areas in nearly 40 years. He wrote then that "From our long discussions a statement of the Chinese position might read: 'We have decided to increase the number of giant pandas and will do so.'" A Chinese proverb says, "Enough shovels of earth—a mountain. Enough pails of water—a river." Anyone who has seen the monumental ability of the Chinese to "just do it"—whether it is building the Great Wall or a Giant Buddha—will understand their confidence regarding pandas.

China succumbed to the lure of the giant panda cult far more readily than to other foreign influences. Père David went to China ready to convert its populace to Christianity; he left believing it would take 40 or 50 *thousand* years to do so. Converting China and much of the rest of the world to the panda cult took just four or five decades. Giant pandas are everywhere in China: on countless counters crowded with plush pandas, on cigarette packages, on candy wrappers, on postage stamps, on everything

Conserving habitat for giant pandas is essential if the species is to survive in the wild. The Chinese government has taken strong measures to conserve and even restore habitat, giving hope for the future.

(Following pages) Building a healthy population of giant pandas in zoos will ensure that animals are available for reintroduction into the wild should that become necessary. Zoo-bred pandas, however, may need to be weaned from attentive humans to be able to survive on their own.

People have an insatiable appetite for giant pandas. But the cult of the giant panda can either help or hurt the conservation of the species. It's up to us to decide.

that promotes tourism and on billboards urging the residents of Chengdu to work on improving the city's environment.

The giant panda cult has not been without critics. In 1939 in England, public frivolity and media frenzy surrounded a giant panda named Ming, who was much visited even by the royal family. But with the prospect of war with Germany looming ever larger, some people were appalled at the panda's dominance of the news. One letter to the editor of London's *Daily Mail* said, "[people] have rubber-necked this monstrosity until their eyes ached. The sickly sentimental panda plague has infected far more people than can ever hope to see it in the flesh. . . ."

Similar sentiments have been voiced ever since, but the critics have been dismissed as curmudgeons. Others object to the money spent to obtain giant pandas, citing the pressing need in Washington, D.C., for example, for better schools and safer streets, even though the funds wouldn't go to such priorities. Still others object to people fawning over giant pandas, and scientists studying their every move, for the sake of the panda's right to privacy. After the National Zoo's Hsing-Hsing died, a *Washington Post* writer expressed his dismay at people's sentimental sense of loss at the death of an animal they really didn't know, compared to our concern for our fellow human beings. He wrote, "On that same front page [as the story reporting Hsing's death] was a grim story reporting that as many as 98,000 Americans may die each year because of medical mistakes. But I suspect none of them will be memorialized with the same fervor as the Chinese bear."

Hua Mei, the first baby giant panda born at the San Diego Zoo, was featured on the cover of *USA Weekend*, with the headline: "Beyond Cute: Why the San Diego Zoo's baby panda, Hua Mei, is the most important animal on the planet." She represents a successful zoo breeding program, a technological coup in that she was conceived via artificial insemination, and a public relations triumph. Tai Shan's birth at the National Zoo evoked similar enthusiasm. But some skeptics asked, do people who melt at panda babies want giant pandas to be part of nature—wild nature in China—or merely part of their experience in local zoos?

There is also a deep human urge to protect appealing creatures. One youngster in Florida invited Tian Tian and Mei Xiang to move to her state, where there were no poachers. The idea that pandas are better off in good zoo homes than they are in the wild is prevalent in China as well, where wild pandas are often "rescued" and sent to breeding centers. So there is a danger that, with the giant panda population growing in zoos and breeding centers, less attention and money will be devoted to saving the giant panda and its habitat in the wild. There is a Chinese fable about a fabulous sea bird that came to a town, where it was feted by the local leader with special wines and meats. But the bird couldn't eat these offerings, and died after three days. The leader treated the bird as he would have wanted to be treated, not as a bird should be treated. This fable may have applications for saving giant pandas.

Giant pandas clearly look like bears, but perhaps no subject in the study of how species of mammals are related has been more controversial. Should giant pandas be grouped with bears, or raccoons, or the red panda, or are they the sole survivor of an ancient group that stands on its own?

Giant pandas belong to the vertebrate class Mammalia, like humans and about 5,415 other species. They belong to the order Carnivora, which includes the dog and cat families. The word "carnivore" means "meat eater," but these are not the only mammalian meat eaters. Virginia opossums, frog-catching bats, squid-eating sperm whales and many other mammal species share a taste for flesh. We use the word "carnivorans" to distinguish the Carnivora from other carnivores. Carnivorans eat meat or a mixture of meat and plant material—except for the bamboo-eating giant and red pandas. Scientists once thought giant pandas and red pandas were closely related. Now, based on genetic evidence and new fossil finds, they believe giant pandas and red panda independently evolved as bamboo specialists.

Scientists have established that the giant panda is a member of the bear family Ursidae. Besides the giant panda, there are seven species of bears: spectacled or Andean bears, Asiatic black

What is a giant panda? Scientists now agree that giant pandas are bears, not relatives of red pandas or raccoons. The giant panda is most closely related to the spectacled bear of South America.

41

(Top, left) In their Andean mountain habitats, spectacled bears eat a diverse diet of fruit and bromeliads, as well as grasses, bulbs, insects and small mammals such as rabbits.

(Top, right) Brown bears, which may still share parts of the giant panda's range, are omnivores that eat both plant material, such as tubers and berries, and animals small and large.

(Left) Native to the Indian subcontinent, the sloth bear specializes in eating termites and ants, supplemented with fruit.

(Left) Arctic-living polar bears eat meat almost exclusively. Their favorite prey is seals, especially ringed seals, but they also hunt bearded and harp seals.

(Bottom, right) In some parts of their Northern Hemisphere range in Europe, Asia and North America, brown bears feast on salmon when the fish are spawning.

(Bottom, left) Brown bears and polar bears are very closely related, and both are near relatives of Asiatic black bears, whose range overlaps that of the giant panda.

Malayan tapir

Asian small-clawed otter

White-cheeked gibbon

Giant Pandas in a Vietnamese Cave

Fossil pandas are part of the Stegodon-Ailuropoda assemblage that has been found in a wide range of sites as far north as Beijing in China and as far south as Lang Trang, a limestone cave system southwest of Hanoi near the Laos border with Vietnam. The Lang Trang site has produced a wealth of fossils that date from the Pleistocene of 150 to about 500 thousand years ago. Many of the species represented in the fossils still occur in the region: tigers, leopards, golden cats, sun bears, Asiatic black bears, palm civets, rhesus macaque, gibbons, dholes (wild dogs), wild pigs, otters, elephants, sambar (a large deer), muntjac (small deer), guar or wild cattle, water buffalo, tapirs and Javan rhinos. Species represented in the cave fossils that are alive today but no longer found in the area include giant pandas and orangutans. Extinct species found there included Stegodon, a relative of the living elephants, and *Homo erectrus*, a primate very close to ourselves.

Environments in Asia were in great flux during the Pleistocene, with variable temperatures, changing amounts of precipitation and shifting sea levels. Tree lines and vegetation zones shifted as much as 4,900 feet in altitude. Humid warmer periods, supporting sub-tropical rain forests, prevailed in south China for 140 to 240 thousand years ago and again from 100 to 130 thousand years ago. During these periods, the warm-adapted primates moved north. During colder dryer periods, they moved south. During the dry periods, there were probably tropical species trapped in areas called refugia, where tropical conditions prevailed. Lang Trang may have been such a tropical refugia.

bears, sloth bears, sun bears, brown bears or grizzlies, polar bears and American black bears. The giant panda's scientific name is *Ailuropoda melanoleuca*. *Ailuropoda* means "catlike feet," but the giant panda's feet are not catlike and the reasons for this name are lost to memory. Cats can retract their claws and walk on their toes; giant pandas can do neither. The species name, *melanoleuca*, means "black and white."

Gaps in the fossil record left the relationships among the giant panda, the red panda, the bears and the raccoons confused for many years. In the early 1980s, Steven O'Brien, a National Zoo research collaborator, and his team examined DNA from all these groups and found that the order Carnivora spilt into families tens of millions of years ago. Further analysis revealed that the progenitor of the tribe Ailuropodini, which gave rise to the giant panda, diverged from the main bear line between 25 and 18 million years ago. These results have been confirmed by other investigators using other techniques. Genetic analysis also shows that the progenitor of the red panda, now recognized to be in its own family Ailuridae, is a sister lineage to the family Mephitidae—the skunks.

Raccoons and red pandas resemble each other, and are about the same size, but it turns out they are not as closely related as scientists once thought. The red panda's nearest living relative may be a skunk.

Follow the Bamboo

The molecular genetic techniques that have demonstrated that the giant panda is a bear and reveal about when its ancestors separated from the other bears cannot tell us where the giant panda evolved. For this, scientists depend the fossil record. Fossils of giant pandas have been found in caves and fissure deposits in China, Myanmar and Vietnam that are dated to the mid-Pleistocene, less than one million years ago. There are

still gaps in the fossil history of the giant panda, but its origin, based on the fossils that have been discovered, was within a triangle that extends from northeastern Myanmar, northern Vietnam and Guangdong province in China in the south to the southern end of China's Shaanxi province in the north. As more scientific work is done and new fossils are discovered, the picture will become more complete.

According to the paleontologist Blair Van Valkenburgh, "There are a fairly limited number of ways to hunt, kill, and consume prey, and consequently, sympatric [living in the same areas at the same time] predators have tended to diverge along the same lines, no matter where they lived. There are bone crackers, meat specialists, and omnivores." These ecospaces have been or are occupied by some type of carnivore or another. But there is yet another ecospace: extreme plant specialist. And a few carnivorans—the bamboo specialist red panda and giant panda evolved to occupy this ecospace. Their teeth reflect this specialization and differ from those of omnivores and pure meat-eaters.

Van Valkenburgh suggests that evolution in the Carnivora is characterized by the loss of generalized features, such as small size and versatile teeth, in favor of more specialization, such as large size and teeth adapted to a particular diet. Once specialized, species rarely revert back to generalists, so specialists may be at a disadvantage during environmental change. It appears that the giant panda moved into a specialized ecospace in which a steady supply of bamboo was the defining resource. This ecospace has apparently been available for millions of years, but if it disappears where panda now live, it is very unlikely these specialists could change their diet.

A driving force in carnivoran evolution is intense competition between species that includes one species killing other similar, competing ones. In the giant panda's range, the omnivore ecospace has been the domain of Asiatic black bears and brown bears. The specialized meat-eating niche is the domain of dholes (Asiatic wild dogs), leopards and, until recently, tigers.

The very first panda-like carnivores, which lived seven to eight million years ago, had teeth suggesting that they were already specialized bamboo eaters. Once such a specialization evolves, a species cannot usually change its diet.

(Following pages) Even though bamboo is very plentiful and available year round in the giant panda's mountain habitat, a giant panda does not usually share its core home range, or food supply, with another adult.

Giant pandas filled the only other ecospace available to a large carnivoran. Biologists don't yet understand why the giant panda has not evolved a more specialized and efficient digestive system for processing bamboo. But there is no reason that giant pandas will not continue to persist, unless they lose the bamboo forests in their habitats to people.

Bamboo is so ubiquitous that the supply seems limitless. Unlike typical grasses that flower and produce seeds annually, most woody bamboo species flower gregariously, produce seeds and then die at irregular intervals but at the same time throughout their range. Most, but not all, members of a species flower and die simultaneously; in one giant panda reserve, only about 10 percent of the bamboo survived after flowering. Depending on the species, bamboos flower and die at intervals from three to 120 years.

What triggers flowering remains a mystery, but many scientists suspect a correlation with droughts, which in monsoon Asia are triggered by southern Pacific Ocean oscillation events, such as El Niño. There are three ideas about why bamboos have mass flowering. Bamboo seeds produced in small numbers over the course of a year or years would be quickly eaten by seed-eating animals, but by producing a huge crop of seeds all at once, many seeds survive to germinate. Another explanation is that flowering all at once increases the chance of successful reproduction in wind-pollinated species, like bamboos, that must be cross-pollinated to produce fertile seeds. The third idea is that few seeds can survive among the dense stalks of adults,

The giant panda's strong jaw muscles power the broad, flat cheek teeth that grind tough bamboo. Depending on the season, pandas eat stems, leaves or shoots of various species of bamboo, for a total daily intake of 20 to 40 pounds per day.

(Following pages) Towering, clump-forming bamboos, which thrive in the sun and usually occur at low elevations, are not much eaten by giant pandas. People use such bamboo, which quickly grows back after harvesting, as construction material and pulp for paper.

The Panda's Thumb

The so-called "pseudo thumb" of the giant panda and red panda, the only living carnivorans to have this trait, is a carpal or wrist bone called the radial sesamoid. This bone is enlarged and functions as an opposable thumb. Both species now use their thumbs to manipulate bamboo, but they appear to have different evolutionary origins. The recent find of a fossil carnivoran from Spain hints at why the red panda evolved its thumb. An early relative of the red panda, *Simocyon*, was a puma-sized carnivoran that hunted on the ground with a bounding gait and scavenged (it had bone-crushing teeth) but climbed trees to avoid predators. Its pseudo thumbs helped it be an expert climber.

so many seeds and the parents' deaths are necessary for the successful reproduction.

In new bamboo colonies established from seeds, it may take years for stems to grow tall enough to serve as food for giant pandas, but a stem may live for 15 years. To spread between flowerings, bamboo reproduces vegetatively via root-like underground stems called rhizomes. Once a year, the bamboo sends up shoots from the rhizomes that emerge from sheaths and grow into stems called culms. Bamboos generally fall into two types: sun-loving and forest or shade-loving. The sun-loving species grow in clumps in the open and can exceed 33 feet in height. Giant pandas live on forest or shade-loving species. These species influence forest succession in panda habitat because their rhizomes suppress the growth of trees, particularly conifers. These bamboos also colonize areas in the forest that have been disturbed.

It boils down to a simple axiom: to understand the giant panda, follow the bamboo. Where giant pandas live today is the northern edge of the distribution of bamboo for this region of Asia. The bamboos that giant pandas eat thrive under humid conditions where there is annual precipitation of at least 60 inches. These bamboos do not grow in arid habitats or in environments with seasonally low humidity. They do not grow in dry valley bottoms or on slopes dried out by cold winds. Where conditions are favorable, however, bamboo responds abundantly to some kinds of disturbance. Indeed, there are extensive stands of bamboo in disturbed southeast Asian rain and monsoon forests, but bamboo is relatively scarce in undisturbed tropical and subtropical forests.

The narrow crescent where the giant panda now lives is uniquely both exposed and protected at the junction of China's two major climate systems. There are no large mountains in southeast China to deflect monsoon-wind driven rains, but high mountains to the north and west deflect the Asian continental weather system's extreme temperatures and harsh drying winds. Moisture-laden clouds are driven northwest by the monsoon into the cul-de-sac formed by the steep western slopes and spines of the Tibetan Plateau. The clouds rising against these steep slopes drop their moisture, resulting in a total annual precipitation well above that of the surrounding regions. The same juxtaposition of mountains and weather appears to have a stabilizing influence on the considerable variation in annual precipitation that occurs in the surrounding region. The resulting climate in the mountains is cooler than would be expected at this latitude, but not extremely so. Rainfall is heavier in summer but the area never seems to be without mist or drizzle, and snow in winter. Humidity is moderate to heavy year round. In essence, the microclimate in the mountains in which the giant pandas live is cool maritime, though the mountains are far inland.

Bamboo thickets growing under conifers on mountain terraces and basins are ideal giant panda habitat. Pandas avoid very steep slopes, preferring more gently sloping terrain, and prefer to stay under a tree canopy even if bamboo is more abundant in the open.

Evolution of a Bamboo-eater

More than 99 percent of the giant panda's diet is bamboo. Asiatic black bears living in the same mountains eat herbs, fruits and nuts, and as a result gain two to three times more energy per pound from their food than do giant pandas. The biology of giant pandas reflects the costs and benefits of subsisting on large, woody grasses. How the giant panda survives as an herbivore with the digestive system of a carnivore is a great enigma—it shouldn't work, but it does. In most of their traits—locomotion, brain size, skull size and age at sexual maturity—giant pandas are quite similar to bears. The real biological distinction is that giant pandas manage to live on bamboo.

Bamboo is a steady food source but its low nutritional value comes with its own constraints. At 11 pounds, the red panda, the other bamboo-eater that coexists with the giant panda through much of its habitat, is much smaller, but has a very low rate of metabolism. While the giant panda's larger body allows it to use bamboo more efficiently, its total bamboo consumption each day is far greater. The larger body of the giant panda may enable it to use the lower-quality, more mature, fibrous bamboo parts more effectively than the red panda, which eats more nutritious leaves, smaller shoots and culms.

Strong competition and predation are forces that drive body size. Giant pandas are outsized by Asiatic black bears and brown bears that share their habitats, but they use these habitats differently. Larger mammals have fewer predators than smaller ones. When similar species compete for food, the more powerful species often kill their competitors: tigers kill leopards, pumas kill coyotes, wolves kill coyotes and pumas, tigers kill

Clouds rising against slopes that
tower over the western edge
of the Sichuan Basin drop their
moisture, creating an ideal
humid climate for bamboo, and
therefore, giant pandas, to thrive.
Mist, drizzle, rain or snow always
blanket this region.

The cold-adapted mountain giant panda finds it much easier to stay warm in winter than cool in the summer.

wolves where they co-occur. A large body coupled with massive bamboo-crushing jaws should deter most predators, such as leopards and dholes, but there is one record of a sub-adult giant panda being killed by a leopard and there are reports of aggressive encounters between dholes and giant pandas. Leopards kill sloth bears in Sri Lanka and other areas of the Indian subcontinent where they co-occur, and an Amur (Siberian) tiger reportedly specialized in killing and eating subadult brown bears in the Russian Far East. Tigers have been extirpated where giant pandas live, but they once may have posed a threat to giant pandas.

The Body Plan

The body plans of mammals are determined largely by the demands of support, locomotion and feeding. Compared with bears of similar weight, giant pandas are shorter and stockier. The trunk of the giant panda is relatively shorter than that of other carnivores. They have four compared to five upper back vertebrae and a distinctively shaped pelvis. Adult giant pandas are 2.3 to 2.6 feet tall at the shoulder. Their forelegs are more powerful

than their hind legs and males are more powerful than females.
The combination of stout limbs and paws and short back
provide strength and mobility of limb movement that create
larger forces over a wider range of motions than similar sized
carnivorans have.

Bears are plantigrade. In all bears except giant pandas, the
soles and heels of their hind feet touch the ground when they
walk; their forefeet are semi-plantigrade, meaning only part
of their soles touch the ground. In contrast, giant pandas have
fully plantigrade forefeet but the heels of their hind feet do
not touch the ground when they walk. Like all the bears, giant
pandas have five toes tipped with strong, curved claws. Unlike
the other bears, but like the red panda, they have non-clawed,
padded, modified sesamoid, or wrist, bones on the forepaws
that they use as opposable thumbs (see sidebar, page 54).

Though they look clumsy, giant pandas are well adapted to travel
over precipitous terrain and through dense bamboo thickets.
Giant pandas move with a diagonal walk common to nearly
all mammals. The walk is bear-like but the stride is longer,
with much more lateral rotation of the shoulders and hips;
this gives them a pigeon-toed look. Giant pandas can
gallop, but rarely do, and sometimes stand erect like
other bears.

Superficially, a giant panda's skull looks like
that of an American black bear or an Asiatic
black bear, but the bones of the skull and jaws
are denser. Giant panda dentition is almost
typical for a bear, with 42 teeth. The broad, flat
molars and premolars, which giant pandas use

Black eye patches, which make
the eyes appear much bigger than
they are, enhance the staring
threat display pandas use to
intimidate each other. Conversely,
an intimidated panda may cover
its eyes with its paws.

to grind bamboo, are larger and more robust than those in a black bear of comparable size. In older pandas, the molars and premolars are usually worn down. The giant panda's skull has a prominent bony ridge, or sagittal crest, above the brain case and wide zygomatic arches, or cheek bones, that form a nearly perfect circle. In other bears, the cheek bones are more triangular. The sagittal crest and zygomatic arches are where the giant panda's powerful jaw muscles attach to the skull.

Pandas move easily through dense bamboo thickets and up and down steep mountain slopes. Occasionally, though, a panda may fall down a mountainside.

Black and White
and Keeping Warm or Cool

Giant pandas are strikingly marked, with black ears, eye patches and nose on a white furred head and neck (see sidebar). The legs are black with the black extending over the shoulders; how far the black fur extends up the back legs and body varies among individuals. Some animals have brown rather than black fur. The white, four-to-six-inch-long tail is longer than that of any other bear except the sloth bear. The conspicuous black eye patches are similar to the "facial masks" of many carnivorans and may function to warn a potential predator that the animal it is about to attack will aggressively defend itself. The eye patches, which enlarge the apparent size of the eye by a factor of ten, may also emphasize the staring threat that giant pandas use during their interactions with other giant pandas.

Not so long ago, there may have been two morphs, or body types, of bamboo-dependent giant pandas: those that lived in hot environments (tropical or lowland giant pandas), and those that lived in cool, moist habitats (mountain giant pandas), similiar to southern and northern raccoons. The raccoon family is tropical and sub-tropical in its origins and present distribution with one exception: the northern raccoons that live over much of the continental United States. To cope with cool northern environs, the northern raccoon diversified its diet and raised its metabolic rate. However, the giant panda could not use either of these tactics when it moved to cooler climates because it is locked into a set of adaptations for eating bamboo. To cope with the cold, the panda could and

Why are Giant Pandas Black and White?

The ethologists Ramona and Desmond Morris speculated that the bold black-and-white markings of a giant panda serve as a warning signal, backed up by dangerous jaws and teeth, to potential predators. Coat color in mammals has three known functions: to signal members of the same species or potential predators; to camouflage the animal; and to augment thermal regulation. After seeing giant pandas in many circumstances, George Schaller and his coworkers at Wolong found that, except in snow, the giant panda's coat did not camouflage it. They thought its function was to signal other giant pandas. As in most mammals, though, coat color and pattern serve multiple functions in ways that are difficult to tease apart. Regardless, the giant panda's bold black-and-white markings are stunning and contribute to their universal appeal.

did enhance the insulation of its pelt to prevent heat loss during winter. But that means that in warm weather, giant pandas face the challenge of how to keep cool while saving energy. The pelt of the mountain giant panda ensures it won't ever live fulltime in a hot, humid environment. The warm-adapted, tropical lowland giant panda is gone, and the cool-adapted form remains.

Senses and Body Functions

The giant panda's brain is similar to that of other bears but has a more specialized cerebral cortex, where higher information processing occurs, than do dogs. The areas that control forelimb and chewing functions are larger than those of other bears. Both forward-facing eyes can focus on a single object. Compared to their large bodies, bears' eyes seem weak and small. Giant pandas have dark small eyes with pupils that have vertical slits, like those of domestic cats; other bears have round pupils like those of a tiger or lion. Their visual acuity is good and they appear to distinguish colors.

The giant panda's ears are large and set well back on the head. All the bears have good hearing, probably superior to ours, but the giant panda's middle ear bones and auditory bulla are compressed, which probably means they may not hear as well as other bears. Giant pandas use their sense of smell to find mates, avoid predators and other giant pandas, and investigate food sources and quality. In fact, the giant panda may use its nose to "see" the world like we use our eyes. To go along with this, giant

Very well insulated fur keeps a panda warm even when it sits in the snow.

Like most carnivorans, a giant panda has binocular vision, meaning it can focus both eyes on a single object at once.

pandas have a well developed scent-marking communication system.

Adult giant pandas examined in Chinese zoos between 1998 and 2000 in a biomedical survey (see page 131) had average body temperatures of 99 degrees Fahrenheit, about the same as brown bears. Cubs have higher body temperatures, between 100.5 and 102.5 degrees. The giant panda's heart rate averages 102 beats per minute. The heart constitutes about one half of one percent of a panda's body weight. A dog's heart is relatively twice as large, perhaps because dogs chase prey. Similarly, all bears have four-lobed lungs, compared to chasing predators such as dogs, that have five lobes.

Longevity and Disease

Bear tend to live long lives, with average longevity into their 20s, but they can live into their 30s in the wild and a decade longer in zoos. Bears die from fighting, in accidents and from starvation when they lose teeth. Man is the single most important cause of bear mortality, killing bears directly in sport hunting and poaching, and when humans and bears come into conflict. Indirectly, people kill bears by usurping their habitat, or the food within it.

The biomedical survey scientists found that about 10 percent of giant pandas studied in Chinese zoos and breeding centers had what they called "stunted growth syndrome." All zoo-born, these pandas had unusually small bodies, bad teeth, gastrointestinal distress, poor coat condition and no sexual development or activity. This condition may be caused by an unknown disease. The biomedical survey also found teeth and mouth disorders and gastrointestinal distress among the 61 giant pandas they examined.

Bears are prone to more than 80 types of internal and external parasites. They are also susceptible to anthrax, candidiasis (a ubiquitous fungi), canine adenovirus (hepatitis), gas gangrene, liver tumors, tumors of the uterine horn, metabolic bone disease, ringworm, blood poisoning and tuberculosis. In zoos, newborn panda cubs have died of infections due to pervasive bacteria.

Challenges of Living on Bamboo

Scientists once thought that wild giant pandas would become more omnivorous when bamboo was in short supply. Giant pandas do occasionally attack domestic goats. It is possible that the first pandas evolved as bone-crackers and at a very early point got forced out of that niche by a more efficient species.

Giant pandas in zoos can subsist on foods besides bamboo, so they could potentially be omnivores, but wild giant pandas are not. If a giant panda comes across a suitable food, it may eat it, but these feeding opportunities are very rare in the bamboo thickets where they live. Wild giant pandas have been reported to eat tree bark, fungus, bamboo rats and musk deer, but these items still constitute only about 1 percent of their diet.

Other members of the Carnivora eat mostly meat or a mixture of meat, fruit and seeds, and digest these easy-to-digest foods in simple stomachs with short intestines because they do not have to keep ingested food for very long to absorb its nutrients. But herbivores have to cope with food that is both low in nutrients

Giant pandas that live in zoos enjoy carrots, apples and sweet potatoes as treats, but wild pandas stick almost entirely to bamboo.

and hard to digest, and so must consume three times as much as meat-eating carnivores to obtain the same amount of energy. As a result, a horse's intestines are about 20 times its body length. Despite its herbivore diet, the intestines of a giant panda are only five to seven times its body length, just slightly longer than a domestic cat's. The panda's small intestine is much reduced, but compared to other bear species, the surface area of the colon is enlarged and characteristics of the large intestine suggest it is populated by microbes that may help digest food. In contrast to the other bears, the pyloric region of the panda's stomach is almost gizzard-like (gizzards are where birds grind up food), but its liver, which aids in protein and fat digestion, is smaller than in the other bears, as is typical for herbivores.

The giant panda, however, does not have advanced adaptations for processing a bulky herbivore diet like horses and cattle do. Pandas retain bamboo in their guts for about eight hours. Giant pandas spend 14 or so hours a day searching for, selecting and eating the 22 to 40 pounds of bamboo they must get daily to survive, but they digest only about 19 percent of that, a very small amount for an herbivore. During the course of a day, giant pandas obtain from 8.5 to 22.5 ounces of protein from that much bamboo. This fills their protein requirements, so it seems that panda eat so much mainly to get the calories in carbohydrates. Giant pandas have opted for one of the strategies used by herbivores living on low-protein plant food: they consume the most nutritious parts of the bamboo—leaves and one year-old stems—and prodigious numbers of new bamboo shoots in season.

Scientists working in China's Wolong Reserve in Sichuan province divided a wild giant panda's year into three seasons. From April to June, pandas ate arrow bamboo stems and umbrella bamboo shoots; from July to October, they ate mostly leaves; and from November to March, they ate old stems of arrow bamboo and leaves. In the Qinling Mountains of China, scientists found that from September to February, giant pandas consumed Bashana bamboo leaves at lower elevations. In March and April, they ate stems and leaves, and shoots as they became available in April through May. In the summer, they climbed up the slopes to eat the new and year-old shoots of Fargesia bamboo. Giant pandas are fussy about which

While resting between meals, a giant panda is digesting its food. It takes about eight hours for bamboo to pass through the panda's digestive system.

Moisture on bamboo leaves provides much of the water that giant pandas need in summer, so they rarely drink. When it's dry, they must drink at least once a day.

A panda, temporarily full, takes
time to rest and digest before
continuing the labor of finding
and eating more bamboo.

shoots they select: the thicker the better, because the proportion of the core to outer sheath is higher. Giant pandas descend the mountains again in September to feed on Bashana leaves.

A 220-pound giant panda needs about 2,200 calories a day to live in a resting state. Energy for growth and reproduction and for other activities raises the total daily requirement to between 3,500 and 4,000 calories. (A person the giant panda's size engaged in moderate activity requires about 3,000 calories.) A giant panda's average daily bamboo intake was estimated to provide between 4,300 and 5,500 calories, a low margin of safety.

Pandas require water. The moisture they excrete is far more than they take in through the bamboo they eat. In summer, their mountain home is often dripping after frequent rains and they do not have to drink, obtaining their water from wet bamboo leaves. In winter, they need to drink at least once a day, but they do not appear to eat snow.

Wild giant pandas' dependence on bamboo shapes their behavior, including where they live; how they forage, mate and rear young; where they hide their young; and where they sleep. In the last three decades, Chinese scientists have collaborated with international colleagues to learn as much as possible about the behavior of giant pandas living in zoos and breeding centers.

Scientists at the National Zoo pioneered studies of the physiology and behavior of Hsing-Hsing and Ling-Ling and have continued these studies with Mei Xiang, Tian Tian and Tai Shan. Other zoos and panda breeding centers have also taken up the cause. But the nature of that environment and the limited number of animals in any one place restrict how a giant panda can respond. Field studies of giant panda ecology and behavior in China, coupled with remote sensing and Geographical Information System (GIS) technology, have added to our understanding of how giant pandas respond to their environments and underpin strategies for saving wild giant pandas. Before these groundbreaking studies, our knowledge of giant panda ecology and behavior was limited to the narratives of panda hunters and to examination of the pandas they shot.

About 99 percent of a giant panda's diet is bamboo. This diet influences almost every other aspect of the species' biology, from the shape of its teeth to its activity cycles and reproductive physiology and behavior.

Giant pandas do not usually move very far in any one day even though they are actively foraging and eating during more than half of the 24-hour cycle. Pandas forage and eat efficiently, wasting as little time and energy as possible.

The Daily Cycle

Experiments conducted with giant pandas living at the National Zoo, Zoo Atlanta and San Diego Zoo confirmed that they have very good spatial memories and learn to forage efficiently with experience. Giant pandas minimize travel between food sites and avoid previously depleted food sites. Although giant pandas have excellent olfactory detection skills, they can use spatial cues, such as the locations of food sources, to find food. They can also learn to use visual cues, such as contrasting colors.

Once it has found food, a giant panda eating bamboo is efficiency in motion. The giant panda's "thumb," used in conjunction with the first digit, enables it to handle bamboo stalks with great precision. The animal's feeding actions shift rapidly and continuously from preparing a piece of bamboo to eat and eating it, without interruption.

Using radio telemetry, scientists have found that on consecutive days, pandas in the Qinling Mountains moved an average straight-line distance of less than 330 yards in winter and about 440 yards in summer. Wild giant pandas in Wolong spent about 60 percent of their time active, but they moved only about 550 yards each day, the equivalent of five to six city blocks. During that time, they were mostly feeding. In Wolong, giant pandas were most active between 4 and 6 a.m. and between 4 and 7 p.m., but the activity times are not synchronized with those of their neighbors. For the remainder of the day, pandas take long rests that usually last two to four hours, but sometimes as long as six hours. The length of their rests is probably determined by how long it takes to digest enough of what they've eaten to make room for more.

Pandas do not make nests, but often rest, or bed, at the base of trees, and they reuse good bedding sites. Giant pandas climb trees to escape other giant pandas or while courting, but they also occasionally rest and sun in trees. Giant panda bedding sites are so characteristic that scientists in the mid-1980s estimated giant panda numbers by counting bedding sites. Panda droppings are found around the perimeter of their beds. After a long rest, between 10 and 50 droppings may accumulate.

Watching giant pandas sleep, boring as it sounds, seems to delight visitors at the National Zoo. The pandas rest on their bellies, all sprawled out, or on their backs with the legs tucked in, or partly on their sides, or with one hind leg in the air, or with their forepaws covering their eyes or muzzle. Sleeping pandas seem completely relaxed but often change positions. While pandas seem the ultimate slackers, they are actually on a very tight schedule. To survive, they must balance how much they have to eat and the time it takes to digest that food—and this is what a giant panda in repose is doing.

Adult giant pandas do not spend as much time in trees as youngsters do, but may sometimes climb to escape disturbance or to rest. Resting under a tree at good bedding sites is more common.

Living Alone

To understand how giant pandas use their habitats, it is important to understand the dynamics of bamboos growing in these mountain forests. The shade-loving bamboo species preferred by giant pandas can grow in stands of a million stems per square mile. Giant pandas live in very thick cover. How large an area does a wild giant panda need to survive? Does it share this area, or parts of it, with other giant pandas or use all of it and defend its territory? How do they communicate?

The Chinese government allowed field biologists to attach

Giant Pandas at a Glance

Order Carnivora

Family Ursidae

Genus and species *Ailuropoda melanoleuca*

Geographic distribution

Giant pandas live in a few mountain ranges in central China, in Sichuan, Shaanxi and Gansu provinces.

Habitat

Giant pandas live in broad-leaf and coniferous forests with a dense understory of bamboo, at elevations between 5,000 and 10,000 feet. Torrential rains or dense mists occur throughout the year in these forests, which are often shrouded in heavy clouds.

Physical description

The giant panda, a black-and-white bear, has a body typical of bears. It has black fur on ears, eye patches, muzzle, legs and shoulders. The rest of the animal's coat is white. The panda's thick, wooly fur keeps it warm in the cool forests of its habitat. Giant pandas have large molar teeth and strong jaw muscles for crushing tough bamboo.

Size

Similar in size to the American black bear, giant pandas stand between two and three feet tall at the shoulder (on all four legs), and reach four to six feet long. Males are larger than females, weighing up to 250 pounds in the wild. Females rarely reach 220 pounds.

Diet

A wild giant panda's diet is almost exclusively bamboo—99 percent. The balance consists of other grasses and occasional small rodents or musk deer fawns.

Reproduction

Giant pandas reach sexual maturity between four and eight years of age. They may be reproductive until about age 20. Female giant pandas give birth between 95 and 160 days after mating. Giant panda cubs may stay with their mothers for up to three years before striking out on their own. This means a wild female, at best, can produce young only every other year.

Lifestyle

A wild panda spends much of its day resting, feeding and seeking food. Giant pandas do not hibernate. Wild pandas have a shorter lifespan than pandas in zoos. There are reports from China of zoo pandas living to as old as 35.

Status

The giant panda is listed as endangered in the World Conservation Union's (IUCN's) Red List of Threatened Animals. There are about 1,600 left in the wild. More than 200 pandas live in zoos and breeding centers around the world, mostly in China.

Social structure

Adult giant pandas are generally solitary, but they do communicate periodically through scent marks, calls and occasional meetings. Offspring stay with their mothers from one and a half to three years.

Development

At birth, the cub is helpless, weighs three to five ounces and is about the size of a stick of butter. Pink, nearly hairless and blind, the cub is 1/900th the size of its mother. Except for marsupials such as kangaroos or opossums, a giant panda baby is the smallest mammal newborn relative to its mother's size. Cubs do not open their eyes until they are six to eight weeks of age and are not mobile until three months. A cub may nurse for eight to nine months.

Giant pandas prefer to forage in dense thickets of bamboo growing under a canopy of trees on gentle slopes. They avoid open areas, such as clear cuts, and very steep slopes, even if bamboo is abundant there.

small radio collars to a few giant pandas. Biologists captured the giant pandas using box-traps baited with cooked mutton, of all things. They discovered that the amount of forest that a giant panda uses depends on its quality.

In Qinling Mountains study sites, each giant panda used on average about three-fourths of a square mile of habitat. In Wolong, giant pandas used on average about four times that area. But these numbers were determined by simply dividing the number of animals into the size of the area. Giant pandas don't divide their mountain homes so neatly. Instead, they live in larger, overlapping home ranges. In Wolong, female home ranges averaged about three square miles while those of adult males varied from 2.5 to four square miles. The giant pandas preferred areas with at least 66 percent forest canopy over the bamboo they were feeding on; they avoided former clear-cut areas, even though the bamboo growing there was very thick. They preferred gently rolling, sloping terraces with gradients of less than 20 percent, which are not abundant here, to steeper hillsides, which are. Furthermore, not all giant panda use their environments in the same way. A male tracked in Tangjiahae had a total range of almost nine square miles because he moved far upslope in the summer, but he spent the winter in a single 250-acre area in the valley. In some other mountain ranges, giant pandas appear to spend the entire year within small home ranges.

Giant pandas live alone in their bamboo thickets except during courtship and when females are raising young. The home areas of both sexes overlap, although it is not clear if they defend these areas in some circumstances. Bears are rarely

Giant pandas eat a variety of species of bamboo, and of parts of bamboo such as stems, leaves and shoots, depending on the season and where they live.

(following pages) After filling up on bamboo, a giant panda must rest until there is room in its digestive tract to eat more.

A very young giant panda squawks loudly and often to get its mother's attention. Later, it remains mostly silent.

territorial. However, there is site-specific dominance among both adult males and females. How do giant pandas communicate to sort this out?

Vocalizations

Giant pandas vocalize infrequently except during mating, but they do have several calls. Giant pandas huff, snort and chomp. These sounds reflect the individual's emotional state, from apprehensive to mildly threatening. Giant pandas honk when mildly distressed and squeal when threatened or attacked. Both calls signal lack of aggressive intent at different intensities. Their bleat call is the only one that seems to signal friendly overtures. The loud moan, bark and chirp calls are probably longer-distance advertisements and are associated with mating.

Adult males bleat to contact and appease females. Males don't bleat to other males or when presented with the urine of other males, but they bleat to the urine of females, whether the females are ready to mate or not. Once a male has detected a female's scent, he vocalizes to initiate contact. The chirping of females is motivated by sexual condition, and females chirp more when exposed to male odors than to female odors. These calls promote social contact. A growl, on the other hand, is an aggressive threat.

Male giant pandas roar during disputes over a female; females roar at persistently courting males. Roars signal aggression at the highest level. During the first months of life, infants squawk when they want attention, a sound hard to ignore.

Giant pandas do not use a range of facial expressions to express mood or intent, but may hide their faces to show submission to a dominant animal.

Body Movements

The familiar tail movements, body postures and facial expressions that cats and dogs use to express their moods are shared by many carnivorans. A giant panda threatens another by lowering its neck or bobbing its head up and down. Opponents may circle each other. Pandas may swat, rear up on their hind legs, lunge and grab an opponent. As a sign of appeasement, a giant panda hunches up and tucks its muzzle between its forelegs. When intimidated, it may cover the black eye patches with the forepaws, like a raccoon does. The giant panda does not have mobile ears and lips or well-developed facial expressions.

A giant panda may roll over on its side to indicate non-aggressive intent. It somersaults and rolls as an invitation to play. Subordinate individuals may be forced into rolls and somersaults, or to lie on their sides and backs, usually

squealing. Given their basic bodies, giant pandas have limited other options for expressing themselves.

Scent Marking

Giant pandas keep track of and communicate with each other primarily through scent-marking. Giant pandas body rub by stroking surfaces (or substrates) with the head, nape, shoulders and back. They scrape the ground with a backward motion of the hind paws. Males scent mark year around; females most frequently do during the mating season. Urine is also used to mark, and females urinate most often during estrus. Males can determine the reproductive status of a female by her scents. Giant pandas use communal scent-marking stations as "community bulletin boards" where several neighboring animals deposit and investigate scents.

As other solitary mammals do, giant pandas leave olfactory and visual signals through their home ranges. They create scent trees by striping off bark; they paw the ground and rub and roll. A female uses scents to avoid strange males. Male scents may facilitate a female's readiness to mate or allow a female to choose her own mate. Other scents allow a parent to recognize its offspring and vice versa, and all pandas to recognize kin and avoid inbreeding. In experimental tests at Wolong, giant pandas detected and responded to ano-genital gland secretions for up to three months but to urine marks for only up to about two weeks. They can distinguish how many days old a urine mark is for up to five days.

Giant pandas lick, sniff and or display flehmen behaviors when they investigate scent marks. In flehmen, a giant panda deeply inhales and curls back its upper lip. This engages its vomeronasal organ through tiny openings just behind the upper incisors in the roof of the mouth.

Body rubbing and handstand urine-marking are used mostly by males. The handstand posture appears to be associated with a male's age and dominance status. "I mark high, so I am old and big," seems to be the message, and other males and females spend more time investigating high scents than low scents, indicating they perceive the presence of a more "important" animal and memorize the scent so as to recognize it later.

Body rubbing, on the other hand, appears to be a way for a giant panda to make its own body odor resemble that of its environment. Males body rubbed on areas with noticeable concentrations of scent marks left by other males, so they may be trying to smell like a territory owner and bluff him. Foot scraping appears to be associated with aggression between males as well as a chemical clue. All giant pandas investigate scent marks they find, but only males and estrous females spend a lot of time scent marking. Male giant pandas actually seek out areas where females live outside the breeding season to deposit scent.

A giant panda strips bark from a tree and scent marks it to create a smelly signpost. Other passing pandas read the messages on the tree, enabling these mostly solitary animals to communicate without meeting face to face.

Mating and Reproduction

A study of wild pandas in the Qinling Mountains revealed that they congregated to breed during the females' spring estrus, which extended from March 7 to April 1, with a peak in the last week in March. Individual females are in heat for only a few days. In zoos and breeding centers, individual females come into heat between mid-March and the end of June. A female that does not conceive in the spring may display a weak fall estrus, but adult male testis size and ejaculate volume decrease through the summer and fall, so whether mating occurs or whether the males are fertile in the fall is unknown.

For a week or two before she is ready to mate, a female become restless, scent marks frequently, bleats often and occasionally chirps. She rubs her reddening and swelling vulva against objects and with her paw. As a female approaches peak sexual receptivity, she becomes less assertive and allows a male to mount. When copulating, she stands quietly, lifting her tail and depressing her back. The male initiates and terminates contact. The female presents her rump while backing up to him or reaches for him gently with her forepaws as she rolls and squirms on her back. A male giant panda has a relatively short penis, and its baculum (a bone in the penis) is short, almost pudgy, unlike the long, thin bacula of other bears. Giant pandas do not have a true scrotum; this has confused some zookeepers as to the sex of the animal in their care.

During copulation, the male squats or stands with his forepaws propped on the female's back. He mounts often, but briefly, unlike other bears, which have prolonged mountings. The male sometimes tries to grasp the female's nape with his teeth.

Intent on mating, a male giant panda may hold the skin on a female's nape between his teeth as he tries to get into the proper position for copulation. When he succeeds and the female cooperates, copulation is very brief.

It is a misconception that giant pandas have trouble reproducing in the wild. Females can give birth about every two years, from age five or seven into their twenties, and 60 percent of cubs survive.

After copulation, the female may turn to bite him and run away from him. Males do not tend females after copulation. As far as we know, females are spontaneous ovulators; that is, ovulation is not induced through repeated copulations and stimulation, as it is in cats. As in other bears, the fertilized egg in the female's uterus develops only to a few cells and then floats free for some time before implanting on the uterine wall.

Giant panda mating seems reasonably typical of mating in many species of mammals, but for many years, zoos and breeding centers were remarkably unsuccessful in producing cubs. Scientist in Wolong found that giant pandas need a pattern of odors to motivate and synchronize sexual behavior and they need to be exposed to appropriate odors at appropriate times to breed. Providing males with the odors of estrous females reduced aggression and heightened libido. Familiarizing a female with a particular male's scent can influence mate preferences and increase sexual behavior.

In the wild, giant panda mating is usually not a matter of a single female and male getting together in a bamboo thicket. The calls of a mating pair attract one or more other males. Scientists in Wolong found that as many as five males may congregate around a female and more than one may mate with her, the dominant male doing so first.

There is a belief among the public that sex is a problem for giant pandas. This, of course, is not so for wild giant pandas; the impression comes from media coverage of the amorous adventures of the few giant pandas that zookeepers outside of China have tried to breed.

A critical consequence of the giant panda's low-energy

Although a female giant panda often produces twins, only one ever survives in the wild.

diet is manifested in modification of various reproductive parameters such as age-at-first reproduction, gestation length and litter size and weight. American black bears first give birth between 3.2 to 6.5 years of age, while giant pandas do between five and seven years. Black bears have six mammae; pandas, four. Maximum litter size at birth in black bears is five, with averages of 1.5 to 3.0; pandas' maximum is two, averaging 1.1 to 1.7. In the wild, only one panda cub survives; in black bears, multiple cub survival is the norm. The sex ratio of surviving cubs in both species is equal, 1:1. The average interval between litters in black bears is 2.0 to 3.2 years; for pandas it is 2.2 years. Average cub survival in black bears is 75 percent and 60 percent in pandas raising one young. Reproductive rates may decline in older ages in both species but they continue to produce cubs into their twenties.

A giant panda population cannot grow as fast as an American black bear population. But the wild giant panda population in a Qinling Mountains study site grew at a 4.1 percent annual rate in the 1990s. This exceeded the annual growth rate found in individual populations of many other bear species.

Giant pandas are not endangered because they reproduce relatively slowly, but their slow reproduction means that a population cannot rapidly rebound after a decline.

Much that is known about reproduction in giant pandas comes from observing giant pandas in zoos, and there have been remarkable advances in our understanding of the complexities of the process in the last five years. At the same time, there has been steady progress toward achieving a viable, self-sustaining population of giant pandas in zoos, so the species will survive even if it goes extinct in the wild. Someday pandas born in zoos may also be candidates for reintroduction to the wild, to supplement a small population or increase its genetic diversity, or to re-populate suitable habitat from which giant pandas have been extirpated.

Reproduction in giant pandas is similar to that of other bears and broadly similar to that of many other mammals. Giant panda young, however, are born particularly small and helpless and demand devoted and intensive care from their mothers. Fathers, as is typical in most mammals, play no role in caring for young.

Some fascinating features of giant panda reproduction include their very short breeding season, their variable-length gestation, which makes it hard to predict when a baby might be born, and

With their secretive ways, giant pandas are difficult to observe in the wild, especially during the months after a baby is born. Most of what we know about how pandas raise babies comes from watching mothers and their young in zoos.

(Top) Born very small and helpless, a panda baby requires constant care from its mother to thrive. (Opposite) Cubs grow quickly, however, and soon need their mothers only as occasional playmates.

the fact that while twins are common, a female almost always abandons one. These features have made it challenging for zoo managers to breed giant pandas consistently and successfully, although that is beginning to change. In 2005 alone, two cubs were born in the United States, at the National and San Diego zoos, and a record 16 were born in the Wolong Breeding Center in China.

Panda Pregnancy

For people who care for giant pandas, the period following either a natural or artificial insemination is fraught with anxiety. First, the period between insemination and giving birth varies from about 85 to 185 days. Second, there is no easy way to tell if a female is pregnant until very near the birth, although scientists are struggling to find one, such as a telltale hormonal signal.

Part of the difficulty in diagnosing pregnancy is because giant pandas, along with other bears, other carnivores such as weasels, and some other mammals, exhibit what is called delayed implantation, or embryonic diapause. In humans, an embryo attaches to the mother's uterine lining soon after fertilization and immediately proceeds to develop. In species with delayed implantation, after fertilization the resulting embryo's development pauses and the embryo floats freely in the female's uterus for weeks or months before it implants. The period of delay is highly variable, but the actual development following implantation is not, and usually lasts four to six weeks in giant pandas.

Scientists at the National Zoo monitor hormonal changes throughout a hoped-for pregnancy by analyzing hormone concentrations in urine, which is fairly easily collected in a zoo. They have found a clear hormonal signal of implantation in that levels of the hormone progesterone rise sharply once the embryo implants. From that point, it will be four to six weeks before a baby is born—or not.

It turns out giant pandas have another characteristic that foils efforts to predict the birth of a baby—obligate pseudopregnancy. In pseudopregnancy, a female's hormonal profile and behavior, such as lethargy, loss of appetite, cradling objects and nest making, are identical whether she is growing a baby or not.

Because a female giant panda cannot detect whether or not she is pregnant, the hormones necessary to support the uterus and fetus during the presumptive time of fetal development are produced regardless—the female is ready just in case she needs to be. Just so, human caretakers can now predict either an impending birth or the end of pseudopregnancy by a sharp decrease in the levels of progesterone, and be ready in case a baby appears a few days later. Scientists suspect, however, that many apparent instances of pseudopregnancy may in fact be real pregnancies in which the embryo dies before birth.

Delayed implantation allows female mammals to mate at the best time, independent of the optimal time for giving birth and raising a baby. In giant pandas, mating in the wild takes place in the spring, when they are eating low-quality bamboo stems and high-quality bamboo shoots. Perhaps the abundance of shoots gives pandas the time and energy for their vigorous courtship activities. Young are generally born in August or September,

Scientists have not yet found a way to determine whether a female giant panda is pregnant until just a few days before she gives birth. This makes the months following a mating or artificial insemination nerve-wracking for human caretakers.

when nutritious bamboo leaves, which are plentiful at this time, give a female easy access to high-quality food while she is nursing a cub. Furthermore, by the time winter arrives, a cub born in August or September has grown a thick coat and is large enough to withstand the cold.

Baby Makers

While giant pandas in the wild seem to reproduce just fine without human intervention, this is not always the case with pandas in zoos. Male pandas often display excessive aggression when they are introduced to a female in estrus, or they show no interest at all. Other males seem unable to get in the right position to copulate. Females, too, may either show no behavioral signs of estrus even when their hormone levels are raised, or they may resist a male's efforts to copulate. To overcome these obstacles, National Zoo scientists and their colleagues have worked to perfect artificial insemination. Although the first cub conceived this way was born at the Beijing Zoo in 1978, only recently has the technique been fairly consistently successful.

In the simplest terms, artificial insemination involves collecting semen from a male panda and injecting it into a female's vagina or uterus at just the right time. Scientists pinpoint that time by monitoring the female's hormones. A peak level of estrogen signals ovulation, and is usually when females and their mates begin copulating. Then estrogen levels rapidly fall; the time when estrogen levels are falling appears to be best time for artificial insemination to produce a fertile egg and a subsequent pregnancy.

This was the procedure that resulted in the birth of Tai Shan

As in most mammals and all bears, giant panda fathers play no role in raising their young. In zoos, males are kept apart from mothers and cubs because males might attack or kill youngsters.

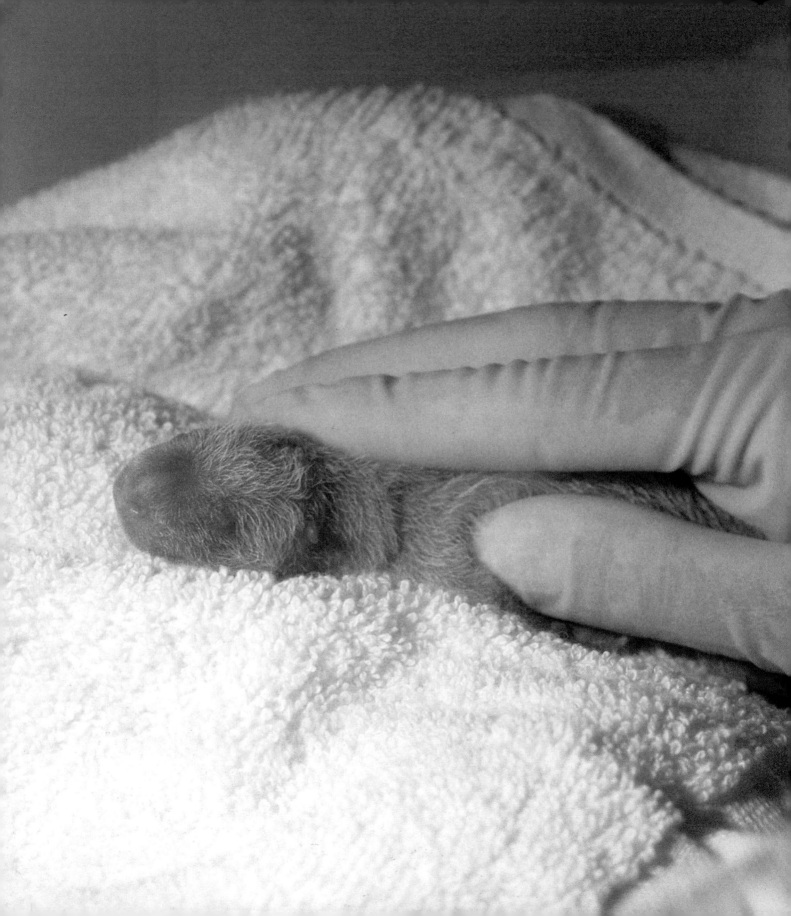

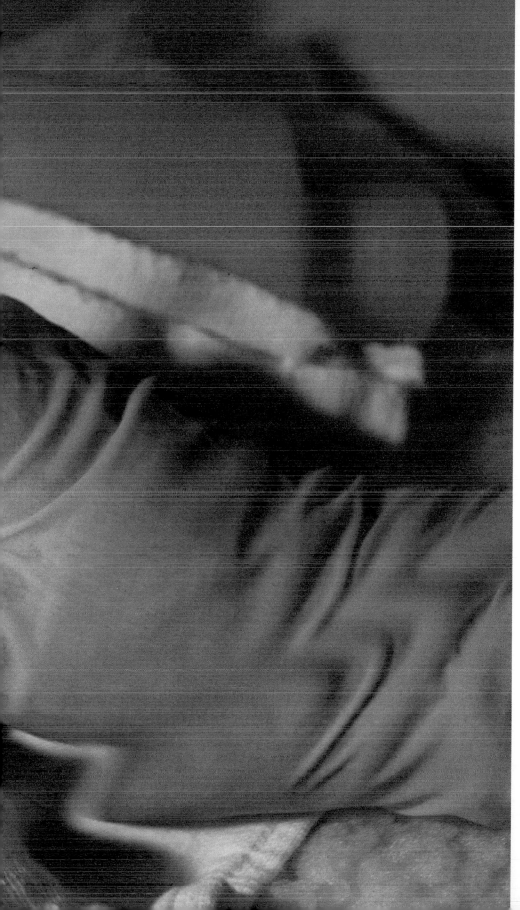

A newborn panda weighs just four to six ounces, is blind and deaf and has just a bit of fur. Its size and shape is often likened to a stick of butter, leading many fans of the National Zoo's Tai Shan to call him "Butterstick."

in 2005. When Tian Tian and Mei Xiang failed to mate around the estrogen peak, zoo scientists and veterinarians went into action. Both pandas were anesthetized, then semen was collected from Tian Tian. The semen was introduced into Mei Xiang's uterus about 18 hours after her estrogen peak. Tai Shan was born 121 days later. Mei Xiang herself was the result of an artificial insemination at the Wolong Breeding Center in 1998.

Apart from using artificial insemination to produce pregnancies, this technique will also enable scientists to better manage the genetics of the zoo population of giant pandas. Managers can "mate" males and females without having to move the individual animals around, and males or females with "good genes" but without an inclination to copulate can contribute to the population's genetic diversity. Scientists hope this will help lead to a healthy, genetically diverse zoo population that might in the future produce animals that can be introduced to natural habitats in China.

(Above) A panda cub snuggles up to its mother's chest to find a nipple and suckle. Mother's milk alone sustains the cub for more than six months.

(Opposite) To move her cub from place to place and to retrieve it when it wanders too far away from her, a panda mother gently grasps it in her mouth.

Caring for Baby

A few days before giving birth, a female giant panda retreats to a den, either a tree hole or a cave in the wild, or a small, secluded dark room in a zoo. She generally refuses food and spends her time resting and sleeping. At the onset of labor, the female become restless and pants. She may also lick her vulva. During the birth of Tai Shan, watchers detected the onset of these signs at about

(Above) For several weeks after its birth, a cub must stay in near-constant physical contact with its mother because it is unable to maintain its own body temperature and relies on its mother to keep warm.

(Opposite) Giant panda mothers are very protective of their young cubs. In the wild, cubs are vulnerable to predators, such as wild dogs and leopards, but a mother's presence will deter an attack.

1 a.m. and the baby was born at 3:41 a.m. At this point, a panda mother begins a big job, as more than 99 percent of a giant panda's growth occurs after its birth.

Within minutes of a female panda giving birth, she picks up the tiny infant and begins to cradle it against her body. Soon after the cub begins to nurse. As in other mammals, the very first milk a mother panda produces is a solution called colostrum. Colostrum is full of immunoglobulin, which gives a newborn some immunity to infectious diseases. Newborn pandas have poorly developed immune systems and getting a good dose of colostrum appears to be very important.

For the next two weeks, and perhaps for long as a month, the mother stays with it constantly, letting it rest on her body or cradling it in her arms. The cub suckles six to 14 times a day, and the mother responds immediately to the baby's squawks and squeals for attention. She carefully licks the baby to keep it clean and to stimulate it to urinate and defecate. She doesn't leave the cub alone even to find food or a take a drink of water, and as a result, also need not leave to eliminate body waste.

In other bear species, females are forced to fast when their cubs are small because food is scarce during the winter birth season. But bamboo is abundant year round and may be available right outside the tree cavity or cave den where mother panda and baby are holed up. In zoos, new mothers refuse food and water even when it is offered frequently and very near the den.

In the wild, a female giant panda never raises twins, although twins are born quite often. In zoos, however, a technique called "twin swapping" enables twins to be raised successfully with a combination of human and maternal care.

Tai Shan Milestones

July 9, 2005: At 3:41 a.m. Mei Xiang gave birth to the National Zoo's first surviving panda cub. The newborn was estimated to weight about 4 ounces and be 7 inches long.

July 20: The cub began to develop black-and-white markings, and by August 1 the cub's coat of sparse white hairs had grown thicker and now bore black markings around the eyes, ears, legs and midsection.

September 21: Tai Shan took his first wobbly step.

October 17: The cub was named Tai Shan.

November 9: Tai Shan weighed more than 17 pounds, about 50 times more than he weighed at birth. Tai was playing by himself and picking up and mouthing pieces of bamboo.

November 16: Tai Shan pulled himself up off the floor onto a ledge about two feet off the ground.

December 5: Tai Shan weighed 22 pounds. Tai played with a toy for the first time.

December 22: Tai Shan, now 25 pounds, went outside for the first time.

January 30: Tai Shan climbed up a tree for the first time.

February 14: Tai Shan played outside in the snow for the first time.

March 27: Tai Shan began to eat bamboo on a regular basis.

April 7: Tai Shan was a very robust and sturdy cub, dividing his time between playing, exploring and sleeping.

May 17: Tai Shan reached the 50-pound mark. Tai was spending less and less time with his mother, the beginning of the weaning process.

July 9: Tai Shan turns one year old and weighs 55 pounds.

September 1: Tai Shan weighs 65 pounds.

The best explanation of this is that the mother must stay with her cub to keep it warm, even though births in the wild occur during late summer and early fall when temperatures are mild. Newborns have only the sparest bit of fur, and, like many newborn mammals, are incapable of thermoregulation. The cub's dense fur grows in quickly, however, roughly coinciding with its mother's first outing. A mother's constant vigilance may also protect the baby from predators.

When her cub is three to six weeks old, a mother is still spending between 69 and 79 percent of her time with it and rarely leaves it for more than minutes. If the cub moves away from her, she carefully picks it up with her mouth and places it on her body.

After this, a mother spends much of her time out of the den foraging and feeding. Unlike some other bears that can store huge amounts of fat before hibernating, the panda's low energy bamboo diet doesn't let a female store much fat, so of necessity she must leave the cub alone much earlier than other bear mothers do.

The first weeks of panda motherhood are very taxing, so much so that twins are born in about half of giant panda pregnancies, but there are no records of two surviving in the wild. Only one zoo female is known to have raised two cubs without human assistance. Unusual among mammals, it also appears that females actively abandon one of the two cubs at birth. In some cases, the abandoned cub is much smaller and less developed than the other, but even when both are about equal in size and strength, the mother ignores one of them. Additionally, in two births of giant pandas at the San Diego

Zoo, ultrasound exams indicated that the mother was carrying twins well into her pregnancy but ultimately gave birth to only one baby. Providing constant care and producing high-fat milk takes a lot of energy. Given the low energy value of bamboo, it may simply be impossible for a mother to keep two cubs warm and well fed.

Why females so often have twins when they can't raise both is a puzzle, but it could be that gestating an additional tiny young is energetically cheap compared to raising one—and starting with two increases the chances of ending up with a

Panda babies develop rapidly. At three months, Tai Shan had grown to 11 pounds, more than 20 times his estimated birth weight, and two feet long. His molar teeth were about to erupt and he was trying to crawl.

healthy one. On the other hand, that one twin is often much smaller than other one suggests that females may not always have enough energy to gestate two of even such tiny babies.

Scientists in Chinese breeding centers for giant pandas have perfected a method of helping a mother to raise twins. In "twin swapping," one newborn twin is immediately taken from its mother and kept warm and well-fed by human caretakers. But every few days, the two cubs are swapped between the mother and the human caretakers. Most mothers, well accustomed to human interaction, do not object to this and the young appear to do fine. Swapping, rather than having humans simply raise one of the two cubs alone, also means that both twins grow up properly socialized.

Development

A newborn giant panda is about seven inches long and weighs just three to seven ounces, although reported birth weights range from 1.9 to 7.6 ounces. Its pink body is nearly hairless. The baby is unable to move or keep itself warm. Its eyes are tightly shut and it cannot hear. A newborn panda cannot even eliminate without its mother licking its ano-genital area, and a good mother licks her cub there and all over its body to keep it clean. What a newborn can do is loudly and emphatically squawk for attention, and a good mother promptly responds by repositioning herself or the cub, moving it tenderly in her mouth to her nipple. During its first weeks, a cub spends its time sleeping and nursing, always nestled on its mother's body.

When a cub is about a week old, black patches appear on

At four months, Tai Shan was a sturdy 17 pounds. He was active, playful and moving outside of the small den in which he'd spent all of his time since birth. In the wild, panda cubs leave their tree dens at about the same age.

the skin around the eyes, ears, shoulders and legs. Black hair grows in these areas in a couple of weeks and white fur becomes thicker until the cub is fully furred and capable of keeping itself warm at three to four weeks. At about the same time, the cub, although incapable of independent locomotion, is able to lift its head and right himself.

At about a month old, a cub resembles a miniature adult although its tail is longer. At birth, a panda's tail is fairly long relative to the rest of its body. As it grows, however, the tail grows more slowly than the rest of the body. At between 30 and 48 days the cub will open its eyes partway and then fully a week or so later. Cubs appear to hear for the first time when their ears open at 31 to 50 days. Other senses appear to function sooner. Cubs tested in the Beijing Zoo first reacted to a sniff of alcohol at 18 days and could tell apart the odor of its keepers and strangers at 45 days. As early as 10 days of age, these cubs discriminated between a glucose solution and a solution that combined glucose and saline.

Beginning at about six weeks, a cub raises itself on its legs and soon after can turn itself over and lift its front legs as if trying to move toward its mother. It continues to grow rapidly and its mother increasingly leaves the cub alone or next to her but without actual contact. This probably reflects the cub's increasing ability to maintain its own body temperature.

By nine weeks, a cub is trying without much success to crawl and walk, until by about 12 weeks it takes its first wobbly steps. At about this time, the cub's deciduous teeth ("baby teeth") begin to erupt. Over the next weeks, its eyesight and hearing become more acute. Finally at about four months, the cub is

Giant pandas, cubs and adults alike, enjoy the snow, which Tai Shan first experienced at about seven months of age. Their super-insulating fur keeps them warm and they seem to revel in slipping and sliding through the powder.

At more than a year old, Tai Shan spends most of his time apart from his mother but still regularly engages her in play.

active, can run several steps and climb on its mother's back. By this time, the cub is nursing only two to three times a day.

A cub's pattern of vocalizations changes significantly during its first several months. Initially the cub is highly vocal, squealing and grunting very frequently. Squealing seems to attract mother's attention while grunting appears to accompany nursing. As the cub is increasingly left alone, however, it vocalizes far less and is usually totally silent while its mother is away. This may be an adaptation to reduce the risk of predation by not calling attention to itself when mother is not around. At the same time, the mother is becoming less responsive to her baby's vocalizations. The mother's licking of the cub, both to stimulate elimination and to keep the baby clean, also gradually declines as the cub is able to

(Below) Tai Shan's first toy was one designed for large dogs. Made of hard rubber, the toy resisted being damaged even by mother Mei Xiang's strong teeth and jaws.

(Opposite) Long before it actually ingests any bamboo, a giant panda cub will play with pieces of the grass and manipulate them in its mouth.

At 13 to 14 weeks, a mother panda may begin to take her cub with her while she goes off to forage, depositing the not-very-mobile cub in a safe place, such as a bamboo patch near where she is eating. In the wild, this stage may let the mother travel farther afield to find bamboo.

But by four to five months, a cub is active, moving around its den and even venturing outside on its own. Initially, its mother is highly protective. She may try to limit the cub's movements and pick it up by the scruff of its neck and return it to the den if it wanders out. Gradually she become more tolerant and lets the cub explore on its own, albeit under her attentive eyes. Mother and cub also begin playful interactions that will continue as the cub matures. The mother may roll the cub around and nuzzle it while the cub swats at her, bites her fur and hangs on, and kicks vigorously. A cub also engages in solitary play, such as trying to put a foot in its mouth and wrestling with bamboo or playing with a ball. The cub's exploratory behavior gradually increases and soon it is able to climb.

Although the cub may not actually eat bamboo for several more months, at four to five months it nurses only once or twice day and begins to play

with bamboo and manipulate it as if imitating its mother. From then on the cub's diet gradually changes from mother's milk to its adult diet.

From about six months to a year, a cub grows steadily and is more confident and assertive even as its mother spends less time close by. This, however, is a vulnerable period for a young panda and consequently it may spend nearly all its time perched high in a tree, out of the reach of potential predators. The cub begins to eat bamboo consistently and its mother increasingly puts off attempts to nurse as the weaning process begins. By about ten months, mother and cub interact only infrequently except for a few episodes of nursing and playing each day. At about one year, the cub's permanent teeth begin to replace its baby teeth. In the wild, the cub leaves its mother at one and a half to two or even three years of age and is completely weaned. This is about the time the mother is ready to mate again and is the preferred age for giant pandas cubs to be separated from their mothers in zoos.

Giant pandas raised by human caretakers and those separated from their mothers at an early age, especially before four months of age, may be poorly socialized adults that exhibit poor mating and mothering skills. This may be particularly true of male giant panda cubs, which spend more time play

(Opposite) Between six months and a year after giving birth, a panda mother increasingly resists her cub's attempts to nurse as the weaning process begins.

(Below) A panda cub's antics, like turning a somersault over a branch, are irresistibly cute.

(Top) As Tai Shan did, a panda cub may spend hours and hours each day sleeping high in a tree.

(Opposite) Without the long period—up to two years—a cub spends with its mother, it will grow up to be a poorly socialized adult that may not breed.

fighting with their mothers than female cubs do even though cubs of both sexes move and engage in solitary play at about the same rates.

Little is known about the activities of sub-adults, those from 19 months to 4.5 years of age, in the wild. During this time they will reach near-adult weight, averaging about 190 pounds for females and 225 for males, and eventually become sexually mature and able to mate. Females tend to mature earlier than males, and in the wild younger males may have less success in the competition for mates than older ones.

Helping Zoo Pandas Breed

Zoos in China began exhibiting giant pandas in the 1940s but it wasn't until 1963 that a cub was born at the Beijing Zoo, to a pair of animals born in the wild. The father of this landmark cub died a few months later, its mother produced two more young in the next 18 years, and the cub, a male, never reproduced at all. Despite best efforts over the years, getting giant pandas to breed successfully in any zoo proved difficult.

Between 1963 and 1989, less than a third of pandas in Chinese zoos reproduced. Nearly two-thirds of the 119 babies born in 75 pregnancies died as infants, and only 16 lived longer than four years. In the next 10 years, there were some advances, such as the first hand-reared twin in 1990, and the zoo population of giant pandas began to grow thanks, for the first time, to an increase in zoo-born young rather than continued infusion of wild-caught animals.

Aiming to create a self-sustaining zoo population, Chinese zoo managers invited the Conservation Breeding Specialist Group

of the World Conservation Union's Species Survival Commission to join their efforts to bolster giant panda reproduction. This led to an intensive effort to assess the health and reproductive status of giant pandas living in four of China's primary panda breeding centers. Twenty specialists from the Unites States, including David Wildt, Jo Gayle Howard and Mark Edwards of the National Zoo, teamed up with more than 50 Chinese specialists to give these animals complete work-ups. This effort, known as the Biomedical Survey, took three years, from 1998 to 2000. All of the new information that emerged from the survey had a profound impact. Husbandry practices improved as did the success of breeding and the reduction of infant mortality, continuing the trend that started in 1990. By the end of 2005, the Chinese zoo population stood at 167, and nearly three-fourths of infants were surviving past three months of age.

Tai Shan spent hours playing "cub in a tub." The confines of the tub may have made him feel safer when he was first in the great outdoors.

CHAPTER 5

Deforestation

Why are wild giant pandas, so beloved by nearly everybody, at risk of becoming extinct? At first, no one knew they were. Early panda hunters valued them because they were distinctive, rare and a science riddle. But rare animals are not always at risk of extinction and giant pandas were only listed as endangered by the United States in 1984, after China began dialogues with the west to identify the threats to their survival.

Deforestation has been primarily responsible for the giant panda's decline. Since the dawn of history in China, forests have been cut, and have grown back or been re-planted over and over. The Yellow River and Wei River valleys were severely deforested between 221 BCE and 220 CE to build dynastic capitals twice—the first capital was burned—and to meet other needs near what is now Xi'an in Shaanxi. Again, in the early 600s, yet another capital was built at Xi'an. Only the forests of the highest peaks of Qinling Mountains have remained uncut, probably due to their inaccessibility. Pandas still survive in the Qinling.

Giant pandas are a conservation-dependent species requiring eternal vigilance. There is no "silver bullet" for meeting this challenge. Cloning giant pandas, even if it could be done, would not help wild giant pandas. A self-sustaining zoo population of

Deforestation over many centuries in giant panda habitat in China, leaving the animals fewer and fewer places to live, is largely responsible for the species' decline.

(Previous pages) Intact giant panda habitat is spectacular, with mountainsides clothed in forest below snow-capped peaks.

(Below and opposite) Lakes clogged with logs headed for downstream mills are largely a thing of the past in giant panda habitat, thanks to recent changes in forestry policy in China aimed at ending logging and restoring forest cover.

giant pandas is a part of the overall conservation effort, but by itself will not recover and restore wild giant pandas.

Protection is critical for the giant panda's survival, but alone it is not enough. Local communities eat away at panda habitat, as does logging. Political inattention threatens giant pandas. All of us can threaten giant pandas if we are not sensitive to the environmental impact of our own habits. Cooperation and understanding at all levels—global, national and within each village affected by and affecting the giant panda's recovery—are the decisive factors in sustaining and restoring panda habitat. The champions of wild giant pandas, and this includes everybody who cares about the quality of life and stewardship

of the Earth, must remain steady, committed, vigilant, adaptive and, above all, cooperative.

Under the Panda's Umbrella

The giant panda's remote habitat is also home to a spectacular array of plants and animals, many of them threatened by the same forces as the panda. Conservationists refer to giant pandas as an "umbrella species." This means that the species' home ranges are large enough and its habitat requirements are broad enough, or exacting enough, that setting aside an area large enough for its long-term survival will automatically protect other species that live under its umbrella.

Most of these other plants and animals, however, do not enjoy the giant panda's celebrity. Takin, for instance, are large golden-furred hoofed mammals that clamber up and down the steep slopes of panda habitat. Beautiful golden snubbed-nosed monkeys add color to the region's trees, while glittering golden pheasants shine on the forest floor. Along with Thorold's deer, which sports huge antlers, and the ethereal dove tree, these species are officially listed as "rare and precious" by the Chinese government. Leopards, clouded leopards, dholes, musk deer and Asiatic black bears are also among the species that may live in panda habitat. Red pandas, too, share habitat with giant pandas, as they share a name and a diet of bamboo.

The distributions of Asian elephants and tigers once at least broadly overlapped that of giant pandas, but they are now gone. People forced out the elephants hundreds of years ago. The tigers disappeared as recently as the middle of the 20th century.

Like so much of China's flora and fauna, snakes and other reptiles have not been very much studied. About 20 reptile species are known to share the Wolong Biosphere Reserve with giant pandas.

(Following pages) Three golden-colored species also live in giant panda habitat, and, like pandas, need protection.

Golden pheasant.

Below: Takin. Opposite: Golden snub-nosed monkeys.

(Below) The dove tree, with its ethereal white bracts that look like flowers, is found only in China, where it is endangered.

(Opposite) Wild irises grow in alpine meadows and line paths through the giant panda's bamboo forests.

Hotspot for Flora and Fauna

The first western naturalists began to explore the rugged high mountains that rim the Sichuan Basin fewer than 150 years ago. They were stunned with what they found: almost every plant and animal they collected was new to western science.

Today, scientists still recognize this region for its natural riches. Conservation International, a Washington, D.C.-based nongovernmental organization, has identified 25 different regions around the world as being the highest priority for conservation action. These hotspots possess high biological diversity and high levels of endemism— that is, species that are found there and nowhere else. The endemic giant panda's home in central China is part of the Hengduan Mountain of South Central China Hotspot.

The Wolong Biosphere Reserve, not far from the Sichuan capital of Chengdu, is the best studied of the region's protected areas. Among the wildlife there are 93 species of mammals, 275 species of birds, 20 reptiles, 17 amphibians, nine fishes and 4,000 plants. For comparison, Great Smokey Mountain National Park in the eastern United States is about the same size as Wolong. It supports about 62 mammal species, 230 bird species, 35 reptiles, 34 amphibians, 85 fishes and 2,000 plants. The Great

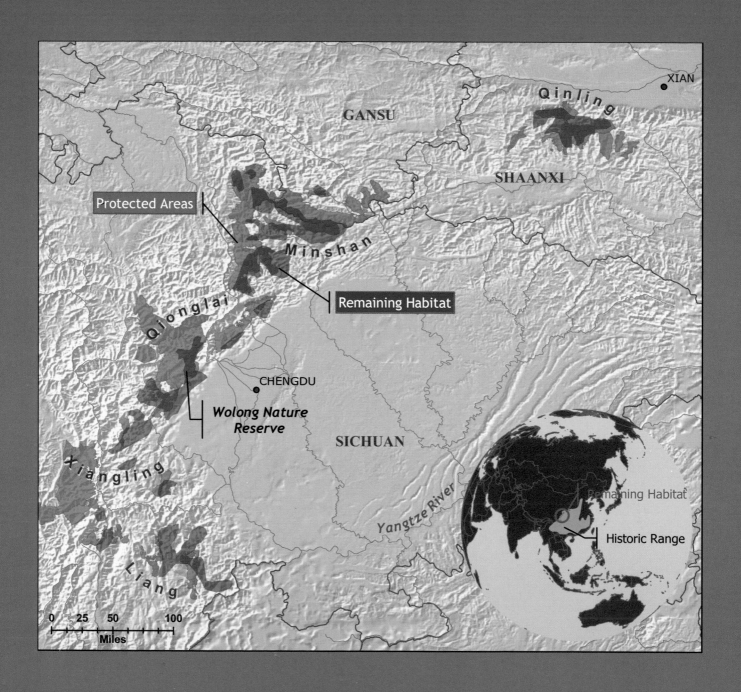

XIAN

Qinling

GANSU

SHAANXI

Protected Areas

Minshan

Remaining Habitat

Qionglai

CHENGDU

Wolong Nature
Reserve

SICHUAN

Xiangling

Liang

Yangtze River

Remaining Habitat

Historic Range

0   25   50   100
Miles

Smokey Mountains are also noted for an immense diversity of mushrooms, some 2,000 species in all, while the southern part of the Hengduan Mountains boasts 4,000 species. Both of these protected areas fall into the World Wildlife Fund's Global 200 list of priority ecoregions.

China's other giant panda reserves most likely boast large numbers of species, with some variation depending on topography and local climate. The southernmost reserves may be slightly more diverse thanks to the infiltration of subtropical species, while cold-hardy Tibetan species predominate in the mountains that rise west of the Sichuan Basin.

Finding and Counting Giant Pandas

When the dialogue between China and the west was renewed in the 1970s, western scientists did not know for sure where giant pandas lived or how many there were. All they had to go on were the writings of western hunters, but the areas the hunters visited in the mountains of central China were limited and visits were abruptly ended after World War II. The only "new" information was a 1974 report called the "Giant Panda Expedition to the Wanglang Nature Reserve." In 1981, however, the Sichuan Bureau of Forestry gave a delegation of Smithsonian scientists copies of a 1977 report showing distributions of the giant panda and some other rare species. The maps in the report, known as the First National Giant Panda Survey, were the first comprehensive picture of wild giant panda distribution in Sichuan.

The Second National Giant Panda Survey, conducted between 1985 and 1988 by a team from the Chinese Ministry

The giant panda's current range in China is a small fraction of its former range, and of the remaining giant panda habitat, only about half is in protected areas. Furthermore, the remaining habitat is divided into isolated patches that pandas can not move among.

of Forestry and the World Wildlife Fund, estimated a wild population of 1,120 giant pandas plus or minus 240, widely rounded to "about 1,000" wild giant pandas. By examining satellite images, the scientists estimated that giant panda habitat in Sichuan Province had shrunk from 7,720 square miles to 3,860 square miles in 15 years, with the situation similar in Gansu and Shaanxi provinces.

In 2004, the Chinese State Council issued a report from the Third National Giant Panda Survey, conducted between 1998 and 2001 by a 172-person field team. The new estimate is 1,590 giant pandas living in about 8,897 square miles of habitat. Sixty-two percent of the population was living in protected areas, which cover about 45 percent of the available giant panda habitat. Giant pandas were reported to be living in 11 more counties than they were earlier. An additional 3,308 square miles of suitable habitat was identified, but no giant pandas were living there.

In 2006, a team of Chinese and British population geneticists, using DNA extracted from panda feces, estimated the panda population in the Min Mountain's Wanglang Reserve at between 67 and 72, a 100 percent increase over the number reported in the Third Survey. If this is correct, and if

(Opposite) Giant panda habitat is blanketed with snow much of the winter, but giant pandas find a year-round supply of bamboo under evergreen trees.

(Below) Giant pandas in the wild are as playful in snow as their zoo counterparts.

these findings apply in other reserves, the total wild giant panda population may be 2,500 to 3,000 individuals.

Giant Pandas, Forests and Floods

Today, giant pandas live only in the tremendous mountains with soaring ridges and deep narrow valleys located in a crescent along the outer eastern edge of the Tibetan Plateau and on its spurs. The wildlife and habitats in these mountains were once insulated from human influence by the sheer ruggedness of the landscape, but the ruggedness also increases the region's vulnerability and decreases its resilience to humans' disruptive influence.

The once-continuous forests in these mountains are now reduced and broken and the giant pandas are in a real squeeze. The lower slopes have been logged and taken over by farmers. Herdsmen burn

Farms carved out of steep slopes replaced the forests that pandas once thrived in. Encouraged by new government policies, however, many farmers are now planting trees instead of crops on these slopes.

The continual expansion of wet-rice agriculture in China in the last 2,000 years permanently displaced both Asian elephants and giant pandas from the lowlands of that country.

the upper forest margins. All that remains for giant pandas is a narrow belt of forest, at places no more than 3,200 feet high. Humans are heavy users of this belt and national and global economies consume logs and other products originating here.

Giant panda conservationists were gravely concerned in the 1980s and 1990s because industrial logging was rapidly eating away old-growth forests where giant pandas live and on which they depend. Then came the floods of the summer of 1998,

ranked by *The China Daily* as "floods of the century," or at least the worst experienced since 1954. These floods caused more than $20 billion worth of damage, affected 240 million people, killed more than 3,000 individuals and flooded 81,060 square miles of land. "Natural" disasters, such as floods and droughts, play large in Chinese environmental history, and Chinese scientists and administrators know that catastrophic flooding downstream during the heavy, monsoon-driven rains is the results of upstream deforestation on steep mountain slopes.

The 1998 floods stimulated decisive actions that have greatly benefited wild giant pandas. A new National Policy Forest Conservation Program was approved and a logging ban was initiated along the Yangtze and Yellow rivers; the area covered under the logging ban was tripled in 2000 to combat flooding. Unlike all the other Asian countries that have tried and failed to maintain logging bans, China has continued to uphold its ban. Since 1997, Chinese statistics show that timber production has fallen 97 percent. A disturbing consequence, however, is that the logging ban has moved destructive logging to Myanmar, Gabon, the Russian Far East and other regions.

While giant panda conservation is a multifaceted, multilayered challenge, it is fair to say that after giving the black-and-white bear the status of a "National Treasure" and absolute

Although poaching of giant pandas is very rare, other species, such as pheasants, are often hunted by local people for food. Pandas sometimes get caught in traps set for takin and other large mammals.

protection, the most effective policy decision by the Chinese government has been this logging ban, which creates a platform for the recovery of panda habitats. Chinese authorities also created new panda reserves, bringing the current number to more than 60, double what existed in 2002. But short-term economic interests can trump a logging ban, as has happened in every other Asian country where they have been tried. The giant panda's wild future depends on whether the Chinese logging ban stays in effect.

Connecting Protected Areas

The human footprint is very large in the mountains where giant pandas survive today. Conservation practice has taught us that effective conservation of biodiversity must meet the complex and diverse needs of both wildlife and people. China's panda reserves will play a central role, but they are not the end-all for the giant panda's wild future. The issues are much more complex than the traditional notion that reserves are like Noah's Arks of natural habitat. These protected areas, in many of which people live, are embedded in mountains where many types of exploitation are occurring, and for conservation to be sustainable, strategies must succeed in allowing people to make a living while protecting the giant panda. Aside from the impact people living in reserves have on giant panda habitat, not all of the area within each reserve meets the giant panda's requirements.

Giant panda conservationists must concentrate on six major challenges. First, giant pandas are tightly tuned to their native habitats, but these habitats are under threat from people living within reserves as well as from outside demand for the resources on which giant pandas depend; giant pandas are at risk while people gather these resources. Chinese authorities have been making progress to reduce these threats.

Second, significant areas in many reserves are marginal giant panda habitat or are made unsuitable by the people who live there. These areas need to be restored to fully suitable habitat wherever possible. Third, giant pandas live in considerable areas of natural habitat that lie outside of reserves. These areas have to be protected as well.

These remnants of natural habitat, whether inside or outside of reserves, are islands surrounded by a sea of agriculture and other human developments. There is a high probability that giant pandas living in small isolated habitat patches will go extinct. Once extirpated from these

(Opposite) Roads crisscross even the remotest parts of Sichuan, creating hazards for pandas and other wildlife and giving access to hunters and gatherers.

(Below) Traditional grazing practices complicate efforts to protect more habitat for giant pandas.

Scenes such as this appear eternal, but in fact change has been constant in China's rural landscapes. At present, there is hope that current change will benefit, not harm, the giant panda.

Livestock grazing degrades even the highest mountain habitats, making them less suitable for pandas and other species. Pandas are squeezed into a narrow belt of forest with grazing above it and farming below.

patches, giant pandas cannot re-colonize because corridors to other habitats with giant pandas have been severed. So the fourth conservation challenge is to maintain or reestablish connections between the core areas where giant pandas live. China's conservation planners are moving to do so.

The fifth challenge is to align prevailing economic forces so that human enterprise can be married to the needs of wild giant pandas. Finally, conservationists must continue to monitor and increase our understanding of how changes in the mountain ranges where giant pandas still live are linked with global climate change and economic globalization, measure how these changes affect the panda's tiny patches of habitat, and communicate the giant panda's needs to local, national and international communities—because giant pandas cannot speak for themselves.

Maintaining Giant Panda Reserves for Pandas

People matter in conservation. A prevailing conservation model follows the dictum "good fences make good neighbors." But fences are tools, not solutions. Many people think that creating nature reserves and national parks will provide protection and ensure the permanence of wildland areas. But there are no pristine areas in Asia, no places free of people and their influence. Many areas called "protected" in China (and around the world) have been heavily used by people for millennia, and many people have the legal right to continue to do so.

The Wolong Nature Reserve, China's flagship giant panda reserve, is a good example. The 772-square mile reserve is thought

to protect about 10 percent of the world's remaining wild giant pandas. However, Jianguo Liu and graduate students from Michigan State University and scientists from the Chinese Academy of Science and the Wolong Nature Reserve reported in a professional paper that more than 66 percent of the reserve was unsuitable habitat for giant pandas, up from 60 percent 20 years before, a change caused by people living in the reserve. Local people have been directly responsible for the destruction of giant panda habitat. Indeed, in the Qionglai Mountains as a whole, only about 20 percent of the total area is suitable for giant pandas and only 40 percent of the land in the other panda reserves is suitable.

In this 2001 study as well as others, Liu's team has described the root causes of this decline. Between 1975 and 1996, the number of people living in the Wolong reserve increased by 66 percent; the number of households increased by 150 percent. The labor force (people 20 to 59 years of age) increased by 45 percent between 1982 and 1996, much faster than the total population. In the past, people living in some reserves either had been moved out or relocated to areas within the reserve where they would have less impact. Both approaches were attempted in Wolong, but the local people did not think they could subsist on what was offered them and, understandably, did not move. The number of people living in the reserve continued to grow.

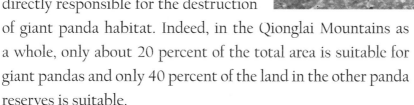

(Opposite) Spectacular scenery attracts tourists to panda country. Carefully managed tourism brings revenue to people living there, creating an incentive for conservation. Uncontrolled, though, tourism can be detrimental to wildlife and wild places.

(Above) The future of people in remote Chinese villages is tied to the pandas that live practically in their backyards, as well as to the global village to which they now belong.

Lilies are among the many ornamental plants that hail from China. In fact, many garden daylilies came to the Unites States from China within the last 100 years. Daylilies abound around Chinese homes, just as they do in parts of the U.S.

Liu and his team used computer simulations to see what might happen if, through improved education and incentives, young people left the area. They found that if only 22 percent relocated, the number of people living in the reserve would decline from 4,300 to 700 by the year 2047. Giant panda habitat would recover, and then increase by seven percent. However, under the status quo, giant panda habitat would be reduced by another 40 percent by 2047.

The team also found that young people would move out of the reserve if they could get a higher education or more job opportunities, and young people had strong family support to do so. The message to conservationists is that education programs that emphasize awareness, protection and participation are all well and good but they will not relieve the human pressure on giant panda habitat in reserves. This will come only through training that readies young people for jobs in a rapidly changing world and working with the business sector to find suitable jobs for them. We have yet to see what policy direction China will take: encourage people to relocate from the panda reserves and begin the recovery of giant panda habitat in Wolong or continue the status quo and lose the habitat so that no giant pandas will remain in the wild there.

One Village at a Time

Conservationists struggle with the challenge of aligning economic forces with conservation. The principal threats to giant panda reserves are firewood collecting, logging, gathering forest products such as mushrooms, tourism, poaching, agriculture, grazing and mining. At least for now, commercial

Giant panda reserves and local people are joining forces to generate income for both. Traditional arts and crafts (top left), sustainable harvest of bamboo, mushrooms and herbs (top right) and bee-keeping for honey are among the new economic activities. Women often play the lead role in these endeavors.

Chinese people harvest thousands of medicinal and food plants, many of them from panda habitat, where foraging activities may disturb the animals.

If children like this youngster grow up and leave the farm for better opportunities in urban areas, the steady loss of panda habitat to growing farm populations can be curtailed.

logging is not a principal threat, but tree cutting for fuel wood and housing construction is. With the heavy penalties that have been imposed, selling a poached giant panda pelt is very risky. Deliberate poaching is not the threat it was in the past, but giant pandas still are sometime snared by hunters seeking other prey.

Ultimately, human values will determine whether we sustain giant panda landscapes. People will always put their own needs and the needs of their families and communities first. To secure a future for giant pandas, conservation actions must be adaptable, relevant and made socially acceptable by linking the welfare of pandas to that of people who live near them. A better future for all of us lies in establishing sustainable relationships between people and resources.

Social scientists have tried to devise some principles that policy makers can apply to enable people to use resources without destroying them. There must be rules about how and how much of a resource can be used that are compatible with ecological conditions. There must be accountability, monitoring and graduated sanctions for violations and low-cost mechanisms for conflict resolution. The China Natural Forest Conservation Program has been complemented with the Grain-for-Green policy (Returning Steep Agricultural Slopes to Forest Program), which is restoring

Growing corn and other crops on steep mountain slopes contributed to erosion caused by loss of forest cover. This in turn has caused disastrous floods.

logged-over areas and reforesting erosion-prone hillsides. This covers nearly 3,000 square miles of land in Sichuan alone. Farmers receive a cash subsidy proportional to the amount of farmland converted to forest. Local communities receive grain subsidies and seedlings for planting plantations and natural forests. These policies will turn tree-cutters into tree-planters and can make a profound difference in securing the future for giant pandas.

The Zoo Connections

Giant pandas living in zoos and breeding centers provide scientists a window through which to discover more. This setting does not allow scientists to examine the panda's complex interactions with other animals and plants, but they have gained a fuller understanding of climatic tolerances, stages in their life history, quality and quantity of resources needed, diseases and a host of other physiological adaptations. By studying giant pandas in zoos, scientists also work to improve pandas' zoo environments.

Giant pandas have been studied in the wild in only a few places, but because some wild giant pandas now live in zoos, scientists have sampled them to explore the genetic structure of pandas in the six isolated mountain ranges. Scientists have used samples from zoo pandas' feces and scent marks to identify individuals, a technology that can now be used to census wild populations. Genetic sampling has also established paternity, which is important when a female became pregnant after both natural mating and artificial insemination and sperm from two different males were involved.

(P.168-169) Corn, or maize, arrived in China from the New World about 450 years ago. It is now a staple among people living in the mountains of central China.

(Opposite) Giant pandas in zoos entertain and educate visitors while giving scientists an opportunity to study aspects of the species' biology that would be difficult or impossible to study in the wild.

Scientists first compiled an ethogram, a catalogue of all behaviors giant pandas display, by watching zoo animals. National Zoo scientist Devra Kleiman published the first giant panda ethogram in 1983 and, slightly expanded, it has been used to this day. Experiments with the giant panda's chemical signals at the Wolong breeding center showed the sophistication of their chemical communication systems. Scientists used detailed studies of zoo-living giant pandas to design environmental enrichment programs to reduce abnormal behaviors, encourage behavioral diversity and promote well-being. Zoo scientists have also developed methods to train a mother to accept a cub she initially rejected. Other training teaches zoo pandas to accept some veterinary procedures without anesthesia.

The Studbook

By tracking all giant pandas living in zoos and breeding centers, scientist have learned much about panda population biology, such as the rate of increase in the population under varying conditions and the factors that control the size of the zoo populations. Zoo managers maintain the *International Studbook for Giant Panda*, published yearly by the Chinese Association of Zoological Parks in cooperation with the International Species Inventory System.

In the studbook, every giant panda has its own number, and all are listed by name, sex, locations where they have lived (different zoos and breeding centers), when and where they were born, their mother and father (or the date they came into the zoo from the wild) and their permanently implanted transponder number so that individuals can be tracked. The

Every giant panda born in a zoo or captured from the wild since 1936, including the Zoo's Tai Shan, is recorded in the *International Studbook for Giant Pandas.* With this detailed record, scientists can track the genetic relationships among the animals.

People caused giant pandas to become endangered, and only people, through changes in their lifestyles and habits, can ensure that these magnificent beloved animals survive in the wild long into the future.

and non-timber forest products such as mushrooms and honey; creating conditions that promote ecotourism; and managing the protected area with input of local people. In Pingwu County, the need for watershed protection, the needs of giant pandas and the very real needs of people are recognized, and the underlying economic well-being of Pingwu County is supported. The Pingwu model will need to be replicated in about 40 more counties across giant panda land, so giant pandas can be stars in ecological recovery as well as an economic success.

A New Day for Pandas

China has made a commitment to the future of giant pandas and so has much of the rest of the world. The giant panda is not a highly resilient species, but the activities of people in its range are the root cause of the giant panda's plight, not its unique adaptations to a diet of bamboo. The conservation challenge is to ensure its ecological needs are met in its spectacular mountain landscapes. If and when we do, the giant panda will persist. The giant panda is a long-term survivor, and it is up to us to decide whether our future will contain a grass-eating bear. Science, programs and policies alone will not save pandas. People will. There is room for everyone to contribute in their own way. The giant panda will survive in the wild, if we let it.

FOR FURTHER READING

Catton, Chris. *Pandas*. New York: Facts on File, Inc., 1990.

Croke, Vicki Constantine. *The Lady and the Panda*. New York: Random House, 2005.

Friends of the National Zoo. *Panda Cam: A Nation Watches Tai Shan the Panda Cub Grow*. New York: Simon and Schuster, 2006.

Lindburg, Donald, and Karen Baragona, eds. *Giant Pandas: Biology and Conservation*. Berkeley: University of California Press, 2004.

Lumpkin, Susan, and John Seidensticker. *Smithsonian Book of Giant Pandas*. Washington D.C.: Smithsonian Institution Press, 2002.

Lu, Zhi, and George B. Schaller. *Giant Pandas in the Wild: Saving an Endangered Species*. New York: Aperture, 2002.

Maple, Terry L. *Saving the Giant Panda*. Atlanta: Longstreet Press, 2001.

Morris, Desmond, and Ramona Morris (revised by Jonathan Baarzdo). *The Giant Panda*. New York: Penguin Books, 1981.

Schaller, George B., Hu Jinchu, Pan Wenshi and Jing Zhu. *The Giant Pandas of Wolong*. Chicago: University of Chicago Press, 1985.

Schaller, George B. *The Last Panda*. Chicago: University of Chicago Press, 1993.

Warren, Lynn. "Panda, Inc." *National Geographic* 210 (1): 42-59.

Wildt, David E, Anju Zhang, Hemin Zhang, Donald L. Janssen and Susie Ellis, eds. *Giant Pandas: Biology, Veterinary Medicine and Management*. Cambridge: Cambridge University Press, 2006.

Sources and suggested readings by chapter are listed at: www.johnseidensticker.com

Smithsonian Resources

Smithsonian web sites that feature giant pandas:

> http://nationalzoo.si.edu/
> http://nationalzoo.si.edu/Animals/Giant Pandas/
> http://nationalzoo.si.edu/Publications/ZooGoer/
> http://www.smithsonianmagazine.com
> http://www.mnh.si.edu/mammals

Visit the Fujifilm Giant Panda Habitat and Asia Trail at the Smithsonian's National Zoological Park.

GIANT PANDAS IN ZOOS AROUND THE WORLD

(as of 2005)

North America

Chapultepec Zoological Park, Mexico City, Mexico: 3 females

Memphis Zoological Garden and Aquarium, Memphis, Tennessee: 1 male, 1 female

National Zoological Park, Washington, D.C., 2 males, 1 female

San Diego Zoological Garden, San Diego, California: 2 males, 2 females

Zoo Atlanta, Atlanta, Georgia, 1 male, 1 female

Europe

Schoenbrunner Tiergarten, Vienna, Austria: 1 male, 1 female

Zoologischer Garten Berlin, Berlin, Germany: 1 male, 1 female

Asia (except China)

Adventure World, Nishimuho-Gun, Wakayama, Japan: 4 males, 2 females

Chiangmai Zoological Garden, Chiangmai, Thailand: 1 male, 1 female

Kobe Oji Zoo, Kobe-Shi, Hyogo, Japan: 1 male, 1 female

Ueno Zoological Gardens, Taito-Ku, Tokyo, Japan: 1 male

China

Baoding Zoo, Baoding, Hebei, China: 1 female

Beijing Zoological Gardens, Beijing, China: 4 males, 4 females

Chengdu Wild Animal Park, Chengdu, Sichuan, China: 1 male

Chengdu Zoological Garden, Chengdu, Sichuan, China: 13 males, 21 females

Chongqing Zoological Garden, Chongqing, China: 1 male, 4 females

Dalian Forest Zoo, Dalian City, Liaoning, China: 1 female

Fuzhou Giant Panda Breeding Center, Fuzhou, Fujian, China: 2 males, 3 females

Guangzhou Zoological Garden, Guangzhou, Guangdong, China: 1 male

Hangzhou Zoological Garden, Hangzhou, Zhejiang, China: 1 female

Hefei Wild Animal Park, Hefei, Anhui, China: 1 female

Jinan Zoo, Jinan, Shandong, China: 1 female

Lanzhou Zoo, Lanzhou, Gansu, China: 1 male

Ocean Park, Aberdeen, Hong Kong, China: 1 male, 1 female

Panyu Xiangjiang Safari Park, Guangzhou, Guangdong, China: 2 females

Qingdao Wild Animal World, Qingdao, Shandong, China: 1 female

Shanghai Wild Animal Park, Shanghai, China: 1 male, 2 females

Shanghai Zoological Garden, Shanghai, China: 1 male

Shanxi Rare Wildlife Save and Research Center, Shanxi, China: 3 males, 6 females

Shenyang Wild Animal Park, Shenyang, Liaoning, China: 1 male

Shenzhen Safari Park, Shenzhen, Guangdong, China: 1 female

Tianjin Zoological Park, Tianjin, China: 2 females

Wolong Nature Reserve of the Giant Panda, Sichuan, China: 24 males, 29 females

Wuhan Zoo, Hanyang Wuhan, Hubei, China: 1 female

Xian Qinling Wild Animal Park, Xian, Shanxi, China: 1 male

Yaan Bifengxia Giant Panda Base, Yaan, Sichuan, China: 14 males, 7 females

The public-at-large has to be a partner in efforts to secure the future of wild giant pandas and an ongoing public awareness and education program is a high-priority. The public—in China and globally—supports the legal framework that protects the giant panda and is footing much of the bill for protecting the species. Educators make an important distinction between people being aware that the giant panda is endangered and actually understanding what risks the giant panda faces in its Chinese mountain home every day, not an easy task when concerned Americans live on the other side of the world.

National Zoo and Friends of the National Zoo educators have created an award winning online giant panda experience called Conservation Central, http://nationalzoo.si.edu/education/ conservationcentral/ to bring the experience of a giant panda in its own home closer to Americans. The educators designed their program to make comparisons between Appalachian North American temperate forests, with the American black bear as the focal species, and the central Chinese temperate forests, with the giant panda as the focal species. Through classroom activities, online simulations, and their own field investigations, students can

PHOTO CREDITS

Heather Angel/Natural Visions: 7, 14, 42, 43, 46, 52-53, 56-57, 58, 82, 137, 140, 141, 146, 147, 168-169

Ann Batdorf: 4, 5, 6, 11, 28, 31, 61, 79, 114, 115, 121, 124, 125, 126, 127, 130, 173, 175, 176, 179, 182

Erwin and Peggy Bauer/Wildstock: 62-63, 75

Teen Becksted (Courtesy Chicago Zoological Society): 19

Jessie Cohen: ii, v, vi, vii, 2, 8-9, 10, 12, 13, 16, 17, 20, 21, 22, 25, 26, 27, 36-37, 38, 40, 42, 44, 45, 48-49, 50, 59, 60, 64, 66, 67, 68-69, 70, 76, 77, 78, 84-85, 86, 87, 88, 90, 92-93, 95, 96-97, 98, 101, 102, 105, 106, 111, 114, 115, 117, 118, 122-123, 129, 138, 143, 148-149, 154-155, 157, 158, 159, 160-161, 164-165, 166, 167, 170, 180-181

C. Loucks/World Wildlife Fund, US: 144, map

Jim Messina/Prairie Wings: 45

Junko Nakamura: i, calligraphy

Amanda Perez: 33

John Seidensticker: vi-vii, 18, 55, 136, 142, 150, 151, 152, 153, 163

Keren Su: vi, 34, 54, 73, 80-81, 83, 108, 109, 110, 112-113, 128, 132, 134-135, 163

Zoo Atlanta: 100

The editor and designer would like to thank J'nie Woosley for her help in researching the photography archives of the National Zoo; and Jessie Cohen and Ann Batdorf for their photographs. This book would not have been possible without their contributions.